NUYORICAN POETRY

An Anthology of Puerto Rican Words and Feelings

NUYORICAN POETRY

An Anthology of Puerto Rican Words and Feelings

Edited by
Miguel Algarín and Miguel Piñero

Associate Editor: Richard August
Photographs by Gil Mendez

WILLIAM MORROW & COMPANY, INC.
NEW YORK   1975

Library of Congress Cataloging in Publication Data

Main entry under title:

Nuyorican poetry.

1. American poetry—Puerto Rican authors. 2. American poetry—New York (City) 3. American poetry—20th century. I. Algarín, Miguel. II. Piñero, Miguel.
PS591.P8N8   811'.5'408   75-22390
ISBN 0-688-02967-1
ISBN 0-688-07966-0 pbk.

CONTENTS

07658

Part II EVOLUTIONARY POETRY

Part III DUSMIC POETRY

Introduction: Nuyorican Language

For the poor New York Puerto Rican there are three survival possibilities. The first is to labor for money and exist in eternal debt. The second is to refuse to trade hours for dollars and to live by your will and "hustle." The third possibility is to create alternative behavioral habits. It is here that the responsibilities of the poet start, for there are no "alternatives" without a vocabulary in which to express them. The poet is responsible for inventing the newness. The newness needs words, words never heard before or used before. The poet has to invent a new language, a new tradition of communication.

The first choice: my mother and father arrive at a feeling of safety when they find themselves dutifully employed to a Mr. Frisk or the Goldwater Memorial Hospital that provides them with a salary. María, my mother, has been working ever since I was born and she plans to keep on working. She feels safe when she works. She feels proud. She is entitled to honor herself and her husband and her children. María is eager to live. For many years she cut leather for handbags to be sent to Miami for sale in luxury hotels. María was so responsible, so fast, so thorough, so on time that she always got whatever overtime there was. Her boss, Mr. Frisk, loved her. He even tried to seduce her, but María was virtuous. At last she felt the need to leave, I never knew why, but she moved her HOURS elsewhere. Once María found a job in the dietary department at the Goldwater Memorial Hospital, she was determined to climb the ladder. She set out to compete. She took on the night shift: 4:00 A.M. to 2:30 P.M. She never missed a day. She became assistant to the assistant of the Head Assistant Dietician. She worked with precision during many crises. She is now assistant to the Head Assistant Dietician. María's hours are still the same. She goes in rain, snow or sleet. She is important in every way—but her take-home pay is only $135.00 a week. Her live planet hours have been richly worked but very poorly paid. She is into the tense struggle of keeping housed, clothed and fed. She lives in eternal debt. She works to survive without embarrassment.

9

The second possibility is living by risks, risks of all types. There are people who will comply with a renegade's law: cheat, lie, strike, kill, deal, sell, buy, rob, cut, choke. Once there is no respect for the system, the options are numerous but very dangerous. Many rules establish the field of action that is permitted. Whenever one of these rules is broken, there is serious institutional action taken against the offender. You can either comply with the law or grab the moment. Take over a building. Go downtown and argue for the deed of ownership. The Renigades of Harlem are doing it. They risk having to learn how to pipe a building, how to gut it, how to build a roof. They risk in order to construct the life that is happening to them. The second choice of refusing to trade live hours for dollars is a choice of endless varieties. The streets are where the game is played. The consequences of street games are totally unpredictable. If you get caught, you must pay. It is true that when you get caught there are plenty of people involved in the same act as you. Yet the fact is that you (not the other) got caught. You become an example—a correctional threat to those not caught. In other words, the second choice is to get out there on the streets and "juggle" without getting caught. Joey's mother struggles with raising a family by selling food in the park. John hustles coke. Meanwhile the street cliques are involved in a transition from organized street hustling to coordinated alternative street government.

The poet blazes a path of fire for the self. He juggles with words. He lives risking each moment. Whatever he does, in every way he moves, he is a prince of the inner city jungle. He is the philosopher of the sugar cane that grows between the cracks of concrete sidewalks. The poet studies Che, Don Pedro Albizu Campos, Mao. He carries the tension of the streets in his mind and he knows how to execute his mind in action. The past teaches the young to juggle all the balls at the same time. The poet juggles with every street corner east of First Avenue and south of Fourteenth Street ending at the Brooklyn Bridge. Poetry is the full act of naming. Naming states of mind. The rebellious, the contentious, the questioning personality wins out. And poetry is on the street burning it up with its visions of the times to be:

> Now only our tomorrows
> Will tell if that arrow
> of love with a head
> of art penetrates into
> higher dimensions.
>
> ("Sad Will Be The Nights
> If The Planets Will No
> Longer Shine" by Lucky
> CienFuegos)

The poet sees his function as a troubadour. He tells the tale of the streets to the streets. The people listen. They cry, they laugh, they dance as the troubadour opens up and tunes his voice and moves his pitch and rhythm to the high tension of *"bomba"* truth. Proclamations of hurt, of anger and hatred. Whirls of high-pitched singing. The voice of the street poet must amplify itself. The poet pierces the crowd with cataracts of clear, clean, precise, concrete words about the liquid, shifting latino reality around him.

Ismael Rivera is *"el sonero major"* at Joey's house. The troubadour among troubadours is the man who sings the live sweat pulse of a people. Ismael's words are about the island, his mother-in-law, his love, life. Ismael is Nuyorican rhythmic communication. Stripped, Ismael is the clean, unspoiled voice of Puerto Ricans both in New York City and the island of Puerto Rico. He is the passionate historian of both worlds. His record sets the tone of Joey's mother's two birthday parties in one. Latin music presides. Everybody dances. The eyes of those who sit dance. The room is in motion. Exhausted factory muscles ripen into joy. Children watch. The sawed-off dungarees, bobby socks, beach caps and lightly shaded shades move nonstop. Beer everywhere. Nuyorican life goes on in spite of the eternal debt for which there is an eternal hustle. Joey's sister is dressed in

11

black on platform shoes. She spins. She moves to the joy of her own birthday. Joey's mother passes colder than cold beer. I am settled. The record changes. The rhythm is Pacheco now. The children see everything. The risk is total involvement. The party costs as much as it costs. The need is to meet the cost and get into debt wherever necessary. A birthday party must be celebrated. Joey's mother spent her actual cash on the cake. She took the beer from la bodega on credit, potato chips provided by her sister, candles for the cake left from last year except for six that Muñeca brought with her. Joey's mother plans to sell *"frituras"* on Sundays to make up the money. She is nowadays a little afraid of the park because she was robbed last week. Nevertheless, she'll make up this debt. The party has to be paid for because she'll need to do it again next year. She lives by risks and that means that she might be caught. Getting caught means getting arrested in the park for selling *"frituras."* If arrested she'll be removed from the flow of street life. However, to risk and not get caught is the law of the street. Most people manage it. Joey's mother is risking it all.

To stay free is not theoretical. It is to take over your immediate environment. Who owns the building in which you live? Find him out, then deal directly. Who is willing to talk his way through the legalese that puts wrinkles on the tongue? Roberto Nazario is willing. He can chew a Municipal Housing Authority contract right down to its bold deceits. So let's take it by steps. If you do not settle for selling your hours for pay, then you must juggle. If you juggle, you can do it for the moment. But there are juggling acts that can stick beyond the day's rip-off. The Renigades of Harlem, an upper Manhattan street clique, are juggling with contractors, electricians, plumbers. They learn skills as the needs make themselves felt, so that as the work on the building grows so do the native skills of the members of the Renigades. Roberto is on the streets night and day supplying information: where do I get a plumber, an electrician, a plasterer? He always knows. He works in the Lower East Side but he learns in East Harlem. The energies are dispersed but the effort to collect them is on. The alternative is the doing. The Dynamite Brothers (a lower East Side clique) rehabilitate their adopted building. They will do whatever is necessary to own, manage and repair the dwelling. Roberto in turn will chew on a mountain of legal conceits like a rabbit on a giant carrot.

But struggle is a hustle and the struggle-hustle is experienced as a shifting balance. Sometimes you can get away with it, other times you get caught. Sometimes you drive for a week without a license and then you get stopped because the rear lights are out and then you get two tickets in one throw. Sometimes a Dynamite Brother can pull a series of hold-ups and get away, yet doing the next—the easiest pull-off—he gets caught. Roberto is saying legalize your "risks." If you protect your community, he says, it will defend you when you need it. If you threaten the community, it will turn you in. People who build their own housing will want to protect it. Roberto sees this clearly. Communities are united by small actions that return the law to the people and inspire them to trust each other.

The rehabilitation of a building on East Second Street by the Dynamites awakens the respect of the people who see the clique at work day to day. You survive by examples. You survive in the doing. You survive by gut will. If the Dynamites defend the people, the people will love and respect their right to establish the LAWS of the community.

Laws control behavior. But it is a choice that people make. If laws destroy a community's sense of safety then the laws are not purposeful, not if they make people vulnerable rather than strong.

A clique (a New York street clique) is a group of people who offer each other safety. Safety in numbers is nationalism. Nationalism is mutual protection. The clique can be small or large. Large nationalist cliques (ITT, Dupont, Chase Manhattan Bank) protect and define their laws. A small nationalist clique is any city gang that is geographically located in a particular neighborhood or city block and protects its laws. The purpose for wearing colors, designing a flag, or having an

13

anthem is to develop an identity. A city clique needs to have a geographical identity as inviolable as that of any nation formally recognized by the UN. But above all a clique offers protection and a sense of "national safety" for its immediate members. Once survival, street protection, is shared by a group of men and women the next step is to assert their collective will again and again and again. Roberto teaches that to adopt a building is the next elementary concrete collective gesture to make.

Work together and paranoia will be diluted. The Dynamite Brothers meet the Renigades of Harlem and the message is work. The mood is humble. Logy, Supreme Vice-President of the Renigades of Harlem, speaks about the commitment to build. The Renigade Brothers perceive the will that has brought the Dynamite Brothers to 119th Street. There is a force, a pull to cohere. Chocolate, a Dynamite, speaks from his guts because he, when in need, finds help without fear among the Renigades. Shorty speaks about taking over the fate of the Puerto Rican in the city. Roy, Supreme President, speaks about having started the Renigades in 1972. He talks about the growth of consciousness from street clubhouse rumbles to concrete decisions about rehabilitating buildings. Roy explains how the police didn't think there would be enough ingenuity. But a chute came up. The dirt, bricks, metal debris came tumbling down. The police ridiculed the idea. The police doubted, doubted, doubted. They doubted beyond doubt: "They can't do it, they don't know how." But the fact is that the Renigades can now teach the Dynamites how to hustle in the housing survival struggle.

Logy's logic is simple. The Dynamites put work into the building, the rewards for the work are clear: clean, warm, secure housing owned by the Dynamites. No landlord, no check going out to management agencies that do not provide the services they are charging for. Logy speaks the Shaman wisdom of our city tribes Supreme Vice-President Logy speaks the words of a visionary. Logy is a poet of action. His metaphysics is to do and then see the consequences. His clear, clean pride in what he is doing

14

arouses the purest impulses in the Dynamites. Everybody feels the simple love and truth in him—the Supreme Vice-President of the Government of the Streets. The marriage is on the way and 119th Street has married Second Street and the results are a possible coalition government: The Dynamite Renigades.

The next day the Renigades continue their work and the Dynamites initiate their construction. The work at first is slow and there is no existing language to express the feelings and work to be done. Language and action are simultaneous realities. Actions create the need for verbal expression. If the action is new so must the words that express it come through as new. Newness in language grows as people do and learn things never done or learned before. The experience of Puerto Ricans on the streets of New York has caused a new language to grow: Nuyorican. Nuyoricans are a special experience in the immigration history of the city of New York. We come to the city as citizens and can retain the use of Spanish and include English. The "naturalizing" process for citizenship does not scare the average Nuyorican into learning English. But pressures of getting a job stimulate the need to master a minimal English usage. But really it is the English around you that seeps into your vocabulary. Everything is in English in the U.S.A., yet there is also a lot of Spanish, and Spanish is now gaining. The mixture of both languages grows. The interchange between both yields new verbal possibilities, new images to deal with the stresses of living on tar and cement.

There is at the edge of every empire a linguistic explosion that results from the many multilingual tribes that collect around wealth and power. The Nuyorican is a slave class that trades hours for dollars at the lowest rung of the earning scale. The poems in this anthology document the conditions of survival: many roaches, many busts, many drug poems, many hate poems—many, many poems of complaints. But the complaints are delivered in a new rhythm. It is a *bomba* rhythm with many changing pitches delivered with a bold stress. The pitches vary but the stress is always *bomba* and the vocabulary is English and

15

Spanish mixed into a new language. The power of Nuyorican talk is that it is street rooted. It is the way people talk in the raw before the spirit is molded into "standards." Any Nuyorican mother shopping for food in La Marqueta on 115th Street is capable of delivering herself of beautiful, original talk:

1) dame half pound de chuleta
2) aceite, bacon, una matita de recao y un container de leche.
3) un momento Mister, no speak to me de esa manera.

Nuyorican is full of muscular expression. It is a language full of short pulsating rhythms that manifest the unrelenting strain that the Nuyorican experiences.

Communications between Nuyoricans and the city institutions are very strained. It is mostly caused by distrust. Language breaks down easily between institutions and those laying claims on change and newfound strength. Step by step trust can be found. But it is not a balanced trust. It goes on and off: for example, Deputy Fire Chief John Hart is in the East Second Street firehouse protecting himself and his company from a City Hall investigation about a woman who died in a fire on Fifth Street. The company stands at attention. The Dynamite Brothers are standing outside. Deputy Fire Chief Hart wants to know how it came to be that "the woman's apartment blew up in flames after the fire had been tamed?" We are listening and the paranoia level rises as the firehouse lieutenant asks for privacy. First the large mobile door is lowered. We then knock on the office door. A burly, rude lieutenant growls, "Go away, come back later, just go away." Slam! We wait. We are angered and humiliated. But we wait. We wait for the Deputy Fire Chief. We discuss storming the place, stringing the Fire Chief out of the fifth floor on rotted cotton candy rope. We feel the pressure to fight. But we wait. We wait courteously. After a long time, the deputy comes out. We had waited and now is our chance.

Kool: May we have a word with you.
Deputy: What do you want?
Kool: We want to talk with you.
Deputy: Please give your complaints to the Firehouse
Captain.
Kool: We're not here complaining, we want to discuss
some things with you and your men.

The fire bells go off. Everybody moves. The Deputy Fire Chief
has to go. But he makes a date with us. The time is set for
six-thirty the same day. We agree. Later we are asked to go to a
meeting elsewhere so we change the time to six-thirty the next
day.

We arrive. We have been talking a good part of the day
both about the lot down the street that we want to make into a
park and the meeting with the Deputy Fire Chief. We know we
are in two worlds. Deputy Fire Chief Hart speaks English. We
speak Nuyorican. But we're ready to move to a point of
understanding. The first fireman to speak warns us just to be
"out there" and "open," to come out with all our grievances:
"Just let it out, come out and name your complaints." One of the
Dynamites says, "We're not in for a long rap about what we've
done." The first fireman insists that "we have to have it out in
the open." The Dynamite repeats that "the hostility between us
is not the point of this meeting. We are here to discuss a needed
change in our relationship with Chief Hart. The Dynamite
Brothers are ready to work with the firemen, but we need their
help in return. We are not here to complain." The worry
wrinkles fall off each fireman's face. Chief Hart looks astonished.
But we know that trust between us goes on and off. One of the
Dynamites says: "We would like to acquire legal possession of
the lot down the street. We are willing to clean it up. We could
use your help." Nuyorican and English are running neck to
neck. Both sides are being respected. The feelings of both parties
are not in static. We are feeling balanced. The Dynamites and
the firemen move into a coherence. Chief Hart looks at Captain

17

Docherty. He snaps into recollection: "That's the lot the city offered us for a parking lot, but we never got to make use of it." The Chief looks pleased. One of the firemen consents to pitch in and work. All of the firemen finally join in consent.

Two languages have met. We talked and understood each other. The outlaw meets the institution. The outlaw discovers the community needs him! "Our fighting is over and our work has just begun. This news I bring you may be hard to believe, but the day has come where the Dynamite Brothers and Sisters are here to help." (From *A Letter To The Community* by Kool, Supreme President of the Dynamites.) The community feels the change. The people's trust grows as the news travels. The need for finding safety is always present. The Dynamites' new image sends vibrations of goodwill throughout the neighborhood. Kool's announcement has traveled through every apartment on the block.

> We will protect your homes, your stores—protect them
> from being robbed. We will protect your kids from getting
> in trouble like the ones we were in. We will stop violence
> among ourselves. What I mean is that you (the community)
> should trust in us so that we can trust in you.

A new day is born.

A new day needs a new language or else the day becomes a repetition of yesterday. Invention is not always a straightening up of things. Oftentimes the newness disrupts. It causes chaos. Two languages coexisting in your head as modes of expression can either strengthen alertness or cause confusion. The streets resound with Spanish and English. The average Nuyorican has a working command of both and normally uses both languages simultaneously. Ordinary life for the Nuyorican happens in both languages. The factory laborer reads instructions in English but feels in Spanish. Thus he expresses responses to the conditions of his environment in Nuyorican. The standardization of a street-born language is always perilous and never easy. Around existing, formally recognized languages whole empires of rules grow. Rules and regulations about speech are conventions that grow (at first) as patterns of self-expression which become fixed in usage—so that as all of the rules and regulations that spring from street usage become established patterns, a body of "grammatical rules" will correspondingly evolve. The evolution of a grammar is slow and at first always a suspicious process for two reasons. The first is that a language that grows out of street experience is dynamic and erratic. There are no boundaries around it. There were no boundaries around the languages that came together in the Iberian peninsula many centuries ago. It took English a good thousand years to establish itself as a formal, regulated tongue. It takes time to have disruptive, tense, informal street talk arrive at an organized respectability. Nuyorican is at its birth. English nouns function as verbs. Spanish verbs function as adjectives. Spanish and English words are made to serve the tenses of existence. Raw life needs raw verbs and raw nouns to express the action and to name the quality of experience. It is necessary to guard against the pressure to legitimize a street language that is in its infancy. Imposing a system of usage on Nuyorican would at the present time stunt its childhood and damage its creative intuition.

The second problem in evolving rules around Nuyorican speech patterns is that if they do not legitimately arise from the street people, the rules and regulations will come from outside already existing grammatical patterns that are not new but old systems of rules imposed on new patterns of speech. This will not do. The risk is on. The Nuyorican will have to continue to express himself without "legitimate rules" to govern his speech. We have to admit that speech comes first. We first verbalize the stresses of street experience and then later, in the aftermath of our street survival, we will sit and talk of our newness and how to shape it.

19

Get rid of the fruit that is spoiled
before it rubs off on freshness.

(Starling, the cook at Project
R.E.T.U.R.N.)

MIGUEL ALGARÍN

July, 1975
Nuyorican Village
New York City

PART I

OUTLAW POETRY

The street definition of the Nuyorican artist is that he creates everything from the raw. T. C. Garcia, Production Manager of El Teatro Ambulante, lives in the teatro office. He writes his poetry and his newly finished play *Who Killed Roberto* as he administers el teatro with Bimbo Rivas and Jorge Brandon. In the last two decades of New York theater, *Short Eyes*, by Miguel Piñero, is the only production of major critical and financial success. However, street theater is happening all over the city. People come to see what's going on in their lives—"barely filtered" as Mel Gussow said about *America Conga Manía* by Lucky CienFuegos in *The New York Times* on February 14, 1975. "Barely filtered" might have been meant as a rap on the knuckles to primitive artists but we read it as a sign that we are coming to terms with reality. Raw, stark, slice of life, penetrating and pungent are the words used to describe what critics suspect are really dramas that do not alter but merely copy life as semidocumentary theatrical experiences. The same critical attitude exists towards the Nuyorican poets. Their use of words is suspect. The critic doesn't "see" how they can extend the poetic traditions, whereas in fact the Nuyorican poet is to the people what the street fighter is to the crowd. The crowd stops to look, to listen and admire his performance. The

23

street fighter delights as he moves fast to prove his point. He'll throw a left/right to the jaw and if it earns him a victory he has taught a lesson to the people; if he loses, he has proven that to prove a point he has to be willing to take a beating. The Nuyorican poet fights with words. When we as poets come upon a man who disputes our use of words, we are in a match where we insist on our right to make our words communicate our experience. The poet's right to define his words is his tool, his knife. The man disputing the poet's definitions must be confronted. A Young Lords Party member ran into Chino Garcia, once leader of the Real Great Society, and said, "Your politics stink," and Chino replied, "I think your politics are OK." Both organizations are Nuyorican born. One still exists, the other does not. Nuyorican poets are more like Chino Garcia: as the poets redefine their language Chino redefines his politics, thus both deal with what is.

      The impulse to create a language that can absorb aggression without fantasy thrives among people who are in situations of extremities. The child in Martita Morales' poem is clean of feeling and open to the flow of the world as she innocently falls into "asking questions." The child asks, "Mami, porqué tú blanca y papi tan?" as she awakens to her skin. Her first act of consciousness is forced upon her by a family that seeks to bleach their blackness right out of their pores. She is innocent but she is hurt. "The Sounds of Sixth Street" starts in a birth of purity,

> so young
> and so innocent . . .

but as the child gets older, she rebels. She talks her anger out as she releases hatred:

> 95% Puerto Rican and
> Black community
> and the white
> honky-ass bourgeoisie
> wants to take over
> and she fights and she fights

24

for her
ARROZ CON GANDULES.

The child grows into a woman who comes all the way up to the
cutting edge and goes for broke,

> she knows she is right
> she fights.

Jorge Lopez is the youngest poet in the anthology. He is
nine years old but his eyes accurately record what he sees,

> When I dream
> I scream, "Come on
> cockroaches, bite me
> Suck my blood."

Jorge is not a neurotic skinny kid terrified of the environment.
He is a plump meteor of energy who looks around and talks a lot
and gives us all a lot of pleasure. But he is clear about what he
sees and he does not lie:

> Dead people walking the streets
> rusty hands and roach-filled pockets
> waiting on the corner stand
> for a number which never comes.

The purity of the insight leads him to a beautiful moment where
he decides that

> georgie lopez va a ser el DDT contra
> los ratones.
> (georgie lopez is going to be the DDT
> against rats.)

Morales and Lopez confront the outside as they see that
what is going on confuses and causes pain. Miguel Piñero was
like them but his behavior alarmed the authorities from the start:

> Constipated-mind castrated—
> feelin' frustrated—bein' invaded
> by pain.
>
> (La Metadona Está Cabrona)

For many reasons Piñero came out fighting. He has fought for his use of words. He has fought for his drugs, and he has fought when he's gotten caught ripping off a pad so that he can keep his chemical cool. He has fought just to fight because he's angry or bored or desperate or just not letting time pass by without confronting an authority that indoctrinates and betrays at the same time.

Wherever the true outlaw goes he alarms the balance of unjust authority. He refuses to be intimidated and repressed. Often it ends in death. Yet these are the risks from the moment that the outlaw says no to intimidation:

> Fired last week man was I mad.
> I don't mean angry or pissed off I
> was mad I wanted to grab the boss
> and the foreman by their
> red necks and kill, kill, kill.
> So I jumped on the elevator and bumped
> into my case worker who said that he
> was taking me off of the rolls cause I
> was working, and that you people think
> you can get away with anything. I wanted
> to snag him by his $50.00 mod tie
> and kill, kill, kill.

(Miguel Piñero, "Kill, Kill, Kill")

The outlaw can be out there confronting the outside by himself or he can be part of an organized action. Most outlaws in New York are on their own. They find "organizing" slow and disappointing, often leading to humiliation because the general will is not compatible with theirs.

The independent outlaw will "Kill, Kill, Kill" rather than adjust and accommodate to insults and powerlessness. Lolita Lebrón took her stand as she confronted the highest authority in the U.S. and for her love and valor Lucky CienFuegos wrote "Lolita Lebrón, Recuerdos Te Mandamos" ("Lolita Lebrón, we send you our greetings"). Lolita is in jail today for resisting:

26

FREEEEEE THAT SISTER
FREE THAT LOVING LOVING
LOOOOOVING SISTER
FREE THAT WOMAN   FREE THAT LOVING
LOVING WOMAN
FREE LOLITA LEBRÓN.

Lucky invokes her release.

The outlaw is morally free to act, to aggress against authority because he realizes that that is his power: he goes for broke whether it is for himself or for his friends or for his people.

Miguel Algarín

Underground Poetry

Spitting
on this platform
or other parts
of this station
is unlawful
offenders are
liable to arrest
$500 fine 6 months
in prison or both
by the dept. of health

Notice
all passengers
are forbidden
to enter upon
or cross the tracks

tormenting itch
of hemorrhoidal tissues
promptly relieved
with preparation H

if u c rd th msg
u c bkm a sec
& gt a gd jb
learn shorthand
in as little as 6 weeks

refresh your taste
with wrigley spearmint gum
you can help
stamp out hepatitis

this number
can save you
from the tragedy
of an abortion

woolite soaks more
than just sweaters clean
passengers are forbidden
to ride between trains

start fresh
with a bill payers loan
up to 1400 dollars
from household finance

Warning
subway tracks
are dangerous
if the train
stops in between
stations
stay inside
do not get out
follow
instructions
of the train crew
or police

Aviso
la vía del tren
subterraneo
es peligrosa

si el trén
se para
entre estaciones
no salga
a fuera
siga las
instrucciones
de los
operadores
del tren
o la policía

Pride fear
and confusion
are stopping
five million
disabled
from getting
the help
they need
what is
stopping you?

Pedro Pietri

A Prayer Backwards

whose arms
     will we have for breakfast
tomorrow morning?
& whose legs
     will we have for lunch
if the afternoon ever comes?
& if we are not extinct
                  by supper time
we can boil our eyeballs
& have visionary soup
     or maybe the war will
    end soon
& we will have something else
             to eat
besides the indigestible
             after effects
       on the menu
of a nuclear con fron tation

Pedro Pietri

before and after graduation day

you jump first
one wino says to the other
do not disappoint your friends
they have been waiting down there
in below zero temperature
for the past 365 days to see you
practice what you preached
do not wait until it gets dark
the lights do not work around
this neighborhood of oldtime religion
strangled by police sirens
hurry up before the reverend
who showed you where the roof was at
changes your mind with
another bottle of gypsy rose
& deports you back to night school
so you can learn how to count
& jump off higher buildings

Pedro Pietri

Song Without Words

(for Sonia Manzano)

the windows of these thoughts
were blessed with insomnia,
I was still at the beach
a long time after we left
listening to the undercurrent
of your violet emotions,
I heard many flower gardens
whispering excellent music
to the sacred silence
on the breeze from the balcony
of the seven senses of darkness,
I have seen you before
in the essence of pleasant dreams
giving the sky flying lessons,
but it's just a room without lights
the melted calendar reminds me
"I know and I don't know "
I say to myself without saying
as the ocean forgets how to swim
when the wisdom of the waves
becomes aware of your tears
and the fact that the wind
became invisible when it learned
how to speak in tongues
to the rhythm of unending bridges
dancing with the shadow
of the integrity of your eyes
that get real blind to see
what their dreams are about,
so let it be unwritten
so let it be unsaid and unheard
we have nothing against nothing
that someday gets into something,
the highway was not high at all

Pedro Pietri

Ode to a Tequila Head

He only drank tequila
  In the middle of the night
He had no woman to love him
  He only had friends to fight
He had no place to sleep
  To think of work he'd done
And mothers would point to their children
  And say, DON'T BE LIKE HIM

So he found his own empty place
  Within tequila and the night
He'd dream of knights and dragons
  He was always putting up a fight
As they carried him from the bar room
  Trying to find him a place to stay
And sure enough wherever they threw him
  Is where he'd sleep away

And this went on for months and months
  Till even his friends got mad
And they'd say, GOTDAMN O MASTER'S SON
  JUST GIVE IT UP, GOTDAMN!
But all that he could think of
  Was tequila at the bar
And slowly watch the dragons fall
  As he slew them with his star

O master's son, O master's son
      Just give it up gotdamn!
And tell our children stories
      Bout the monsters of the land
And how when they stood in your way
      You wouldn't take the fall
Or turn the other cheek, or pray
      Or cry or finally crawl

I'd like to hear a story
      Of how you stood upon your pain
And fought away the madness
      Of a lonely cold that came
To make you fall and stumble
      Trying to strip you of your name
But you said, NO, I WILL NOT GO,
      And back to us you came.

Sandra María Esteves

Felipa — La Filósofa Del Rincón

Mi mestizo, te digo que
las ventanas donde tú
primero le diste un zapatón
a esos cinco pesos
      /estan muertas.
La única verdad es el
polvo que existe adentro de
esos ojos que tu llama
      "Wall Strit."
      Pero mira bien!
que hay un clavo
en nuestra sombra. Y ahora
que la sombra está seca / me
dice el Times y el Daily News
de mierda que nuestra gente
tiene una lucha Guilladita
debajo de esas sombras. Y
que andamos con unas muletas
como niños sin leche y una
muñeca de Matell.

      El americano dice:
que sus cenos llenan la lluvia
concelos y que sin sus cenos
m e c á n i c o s, nuestra
vida nunca podrá levantar las
mañanas, sino con unos
g r i t o s de infancia!

Pues yo pregunto,
mi mestizo: ¿ que queremos con
esa nieve blanca y fría? Y sé:
que el americano mira con su
sanitation trucks para darles
a los pobres huérfanos un xmas
de nuevo nacimiento . . . para que
se escondan sus ojos y orejas
en unos bolsillos de sangre
muerta y olvidada.

Pues es ahora, mi
mestizo, que yo sé: que en la
montaña de los bosques, donde
viven los indios espirituales,
los negros café y los negros
loango—los mestizos, que tambiens—
GRITAN Y GRITAN Y GRITAN
Y GRITAN Las Cataratas cuando
ellas se t i r a n en los
sueños de nuestra LUCHA / por

t e m o r
que nadie pueda oir nuestros
n i ñ o s . . .

gritando
debajo de
la n i e v e.

José-Angel Figueroa

Felipa—La Filósofa Del Rincón

My half-breed, I tell you
that the windows
where you first
kicked those
five dollars
        / are dead.

The only truth
is the powder that
exists inside
those eyes that you call
        "Wall Strit."
        But take a good look!
there's a nail
in our shadows.

     And now that
the shadows are dry they
tell me the Times and The Daily News
the shit that our people have a
sneaky struggle under those shadows and
that we walk with crutches
like children without milk and a
doll from Matell.

     The american says:
that his breast fills the rain
with jealousy and that without his mechanical
breast, our
lives could never lift up the
tomorrows, lest they be an
infant's cry!

        But I question,
my half-breed: what do we want with
that white snow and cold? I know:
that the american looks with his
sanitation trucks to give
the poor orphans an xmas
of new birth . . . in order to
hide his eyes and ears
in pockets of blood
death and forgetfulness.

        It is now, my
half-breed, I know: that in the
mountain forests, where the
spiritualist indians live,
the coffee black man and the black
Loango—the half-breeds, they too
scream and scream and scream
and scream the waterfalls when
they throw themselves into the
dreams of our struggle / for
f e a r
that no one will hear our
children . . .

                        crying
                        underneath the
                        snow.

José-Angel Figueroa
(translation by *Miguel Piñero*)

                            40

About los Ratones

Los ratones venden las drogas
la cojen—la usan—se meten las agujas
sucias
La usan en el bronx
se meten la coca como se meten en los clubs de
billar
they play nodding out pool
they are behind the eight ball
georgie lopez va a ser el DDT contra
los ratones
se meten en los basements
con una ganga de erba y coca
Los ratones le venden a los viejos y
las viejas y a los young people like
me, georgie lopez
pero georgie lopez es el DDT contra
los ratones
yo soy el rat poison que se mete en las
esquinas de las esquinas de las calles
oh man, yeah, man sí there are mucho rats
and we need more cats
los gatos will tener una guerra contra los
ratones very soon
yo sé, yo sé, porque yo soy
georgie lopez DDT contra los
Ratones

Jorge Lopez

41

About the Rats

The rats sell drugs
they take it—they use it—
they stick themselves with dirty
needles
They use it in the Bronx
they get into cocaine like they get into
the billiard clubs
they play nodding out pool
they are behind the eight ball
georgie lopez will be the DDT against
the rats
they get into the basements
with a gang of grass and coke
The rats sell to old men
old ladies and to young people like
me georgie lopez
But georgie lopez is the DDT against
the rats
I am the rat poison that will get into
the corner of the corner of the streets
oh man, yeah, man yes there are plenty of
rats and we need more cats
the cats will have a war against the
rats very soon
I know, I know, because I am
georgie lopez DDT against the
Rats.

Jorge Lopez
(translation by *Miguel Piñero*)

Pesetas de Embuste

Cuando yo duermo
grito, "Vente cucaracha
muérdeme
chúpame la sangre,
el veneno para los
vampiros—enemigos
con dientes largos . . .
Vente cucaracha muérdeme
los molleros,
el brazo,
las empollas
contaminate you and los ratones."
Dicen las cucarachas,
"Come
a chupar la sangre de georgie lopez
como chupan queso con pan."
Vienen los vampiros a hablarme
por la noche y yo le doy
pesetas de embustes
porque el pan está contaminated con
traps
Nosotros tenemos meetings con las cucarachas
que son las cucarachas en la casa de las
cucarachas que visitan los vampiros para
chuparle la sangre a los ratones en el 538
east 6th st. que es mi casa y beben
cerveza con sangre.

Jorge Lopez

Counterfeit Quarters

When I dream
I scream, "Come on cockroach,
bite me
suck my blood,
the poison for the
vampires—the enemies
with long teeth . . .
Come on cockroach, bite my
muscles
my arm,
my boils will
contaminate you and the rats."
The cockroaches say,
"Come
let's suck the blood of georgie lopez
like sucking bread and cheese."
The vampires come to speak with me
at night and I give them
counterfeit quarters
because the bread is contaminated with
traps
We have meetings with the cockroaches
who are cockroaches in the house of
cockroaches who visit the vampires
to suck the blood of the rats in 538
east 6th st. which is my house, and drink
beer with blood.

Jorge Lopez
(translation by *Miguel Piñero*)

Viet-Nam

So here goes the story of Viet-Nam.

In 1967, my father joined the
United States army.
I told my father not to join.
I begged him and so his wife did.
So in 1968, my father went
overseas to Germany.
My mother got sad and
looked at his picture
before he left for Germany.
We knew that it was going
to be hard without him in the house.
From Germany they had sent my father
to Viet-Nam.
He wrote from Viet-Nam to my mother's house,
and he kept on writing more & more letters.
My mother opened a letter,
so the letter was saying,
"My wife, it is true what you have said
about the army,
I should have listened to you,
but I kept on.
Now I am going into action to Viet-Nam.
Here I am on my way in a big boat
to fight other people.
These people I am fighting
have never done nothing to me,
so why should I kill them
without no answer
Is it still my duty to fight?"

Two years after, my mother got a card.
She was so excited cause he had written to her.
My mother opened the letter
and read what my father had
said to her about me.
He misses his son cause he is the

46

only one he got,
"and say hello to my family."
She closed this letter with her hands
but never her heart . . .

                        . . . it's been two years I've been fighting
                        through this war
                        I keep on moving forward cause I know
                        I have to make it to the other side
                        to go home.
                        So I kill and shoot
                        throw grenades
                        but I don't want to pull the trigger back
                        to kill Vietnamese . . .

So two months later I got this letter.
When I opened the letter, I got into a shock,
I turned pale because I thought it wasn't true.
So I screamed loud and cried soft.
My father had passed away in Viet-Nam.
But I didn't want to tell my mother
cause I didn't want to break her heart.
Me like a man
I hold my tears inside.
I told my mother about what happened to my father,
she shouted and screamed
telling me it wasn't true.

She did not believe the letter.
So they called up Fort Hamilton,
they told my mother it was true
that he had passed away in Viet-Nam.
We went to the funeral to see him.
It was true, it was my father
who had passed away in Viet-Nam.
So I opened the box,
I looked back to make sure
my mother wasn't there.
So when my mother wasn't there
I opened the box again—

I looked from his stomach to his feet.
I knew something was wrong.
Half of his body wasn't his,
cause I looked at his leg,
he had had a scar,
so it was another man's body.
I knew my father had died
by being blown up by a grenade.
I slammed the box,
I got mad and vicious
cause I had not been told about my father's body.
I kept it a secret.
I didn't tell my mother.
I had the secret for a long time.
Day after night I slept
thinking of my father's body.
I realized when you do go to Viet-Nam,
you don't come back in one piece.
Some pieces are missing
just like my father's pieces were missing.

So heavily after I kept the secret to myself
for a long long time.
Now I go to my house
and think of the days I used to be
with my father.
I wish it wasn't true,
I wish I really had my father
next to my side like other boys
got their fathers next to them.
Now I know I have to take care of my mother
for my father.
My father told me if he ever died
to take care of the family
cause I am the oldest in the house.
I say inside me, bless my father
cause he died in a moment nobody expected.
Well the only thing I can say is
God has him in good hands. Bye, pops, bye.

Archie Martinez

The Sounds of Sixth Street

Kids with innocent minds
and their curiosity aroused

"¿Mami, porqué tú blanca y papi tan?"

your curiosity aroused you into asking the question
your curiosity was wandering
you wondered why all the spanish speaking people
are of many different colors

"Chocolate
hey nene
mira
Chocolate
hey mira
ven acá Chocolate"

but he kept on running
and
you had no knowledge
that
that wasn't his name
but the name of his color
which was Tan or Brown
you did not know
that
the Puerto Rican people
are a mixture of
many different races
you do not know
for you are
so young
and so innocent
and when your mother
would take you to the park
or in the summer
to the beach
where you play in the sand
with many different people

people—
men and women of your age
that range from about 3-5
you do not know
for they are all
beautiful people
because you can all play
get along
and be in a world of your own
but as the child gets older
she rebels
rebels against the fact
that
her parents will not let her have a boyfriend
with an afro
or con el pelo grifo
because he looks black
and black to them is dirty
but dead and silky blond hair
with blue eyes
and white skin
is supposed to be pure
and she rebels against the fact
that where she lives at
is a
95% Puerto Rican and
Black community
and the white
honky Ass-bourgeoisie
wants to take over
and she fights and she fights
for her
ARROZ CON GANDULES
for lunch
instead of that so-called lunch
peanut butter and jelly sandwiches
with peagreen soup

which looks like—CHURRAS
and she fights and
she fights
for what she thinks is right
she fights and
she rebels
and for this
she gets expelled
but she never gives up
no she never gives up
because in what they are doing
they are wrong and
she knows she is right
she fights
and she is in assembly in school
and because she does not stand up
like the rest of her fellow students
to do the pledge of allegiance to the amerikan flag
she is harassed by her teacher and two deans
she is almost expelled
at which she more fully rebels
and they ask her questions after questions
that she doesn't dig so she just gets up and she tips
cause she is tired of being harassed by that MOTHER FUCKING
      white ass
this is a Puerto Rican girl
trigueña and fifteen years old
this is a Puerto Rican girl
      to her, her flag is GOLD
and she rebels
and she rebels
and for this, they want her expelled
but she keeps on fighting
yeah, she fights and she fights
because she knows she is Right!

Martita Morales

A Mongo Affair

On the corner by the plaza
in front of
the entrance to Gonzalez-Padín
in old San Juan
a black Puerto Rican talks
about "the race"
he talks of Boricuas
who are in New York on welfare
and on lines waiting for food stamps,
"yes, it's true, they've been taken out
and sent abroad and those that
went over tell me that they're
doing better over there than here
they tell me they get money
and medical aid
that their rent is paid
that their clothes get bought
that their teeth get fixed
is that true?"
on the corner by
the entrance to Gonzalez-Padín
I have to admit that he has been
lied to, misled,
that I know that all the goodies
he named humiliate the receiver,
that a man is demoralized
when his woman and children
beg for weekly checks
that even the fucking a man does
on a government bought mattress
draws the blood from his cock
cockless, sin espina dorsal,
mongo—that's it!
a welfare fuck is a mongo affair!
mongo means flojo
mongo means bloodless
mongo means soft

52

mongo can not penetrate
mongo can only tease
but it can't tickle
the juice of the earth-vagina
mongo es el bicho Taino
porque murió
mongo es el borinqueño
who's been moved
to the inner-city jungles
of north american cities
mongo is the rican who survives
in the tar jungle of Chicago
who cleans, weeps, crawls,
gets ripped off,
sucks the eighty dollars a week
from the syphilitic
down deep frustrated
northern man—
viejo negro africano,
Africa Puerto Rico
sitting on department store entrances
don't believe the deadly game
of Northern cities paved with gold and plenty
don't believe the fetching dream
of life improvement in New York
the only thing you'll find in Boston
is a soft leather shoe up your ass,
viejo, anciano africano, Washington
will send you in your old age
to clean the battlefields
in Korea and Vietnam
you'll be carrying a sack
and into that canvas
you'll pitch las uñas
los intestinos
las piernas
los bichos mongos

of Puerto Rican soldiers
put at the front to face
sí!
to face the bullets, bombs, missiles,
sí! the artillery
sí!
to face the violent hatred of Nazi Germany
to confront the hungry anger of the world
viejo negro
viejo puertorriqueno
the north offers us pain
and everlasting humiliation
IT DOES NOT COUGH UP
THE EASY LIFE: THAT IS A LIE
viejo que has visto la isla
perder sus hijos
are there guns to deal with
genocide, expatriation?
are there arms to hold
the exodus of borinqueños
from Borinquen?
we have been moved
we have been shipped
we have been parcel posted
first by water then by air
el correo has special prices
for the "low island element" to be
removed, then dumped
into the inner-city ghettos
Viejo, Viejo, Viejo
we are the minority
here in Borinquen
we, the Puerto Rican,
the original man of this island
is in the minority
I writhe with pain
I jump with anger

I know
I see
I am "la minoría de la isla"
viejo, viejo anciano
do you hear me?
there are no more Puerto Ricans
in Borinquen
I am the minority everywhere
I am among the few in all societies
I belong to a tribe of nomads
that roam the world without
a place to call a home,
there is no place that is ALL MINE
there is no place that I can
call mi casa,
I, yo, Miguel ¡ Me oyes viejo!
I, yo, Miguel
el hijo de Maria Socorro y Miguel
is homeless, has been homeless
will be homeless
in the to be
and the to come
Miguelito, Lucky, Bimbo
you like me have lost
your home
and to the first idealist
I meet
I'll say
don't lie to me
don't fill me full of vain
disturbing love for an island
filled with Burger Kings
for I know
there are no cuchifritos
in Borinquen
I remember last night
viejito lindo

when your eyes fired me
with trust
do you hear that?
with trust
and when you said
that you would stand by me
should any danger threaten
I halfway threw myself
into your arms to weep
mis gracias
I loved you
viejo negro
I would have slept
in your arms
I would have caressed
your curly gray hair
I wanted to touch
your wrinkled face
when your eyes fired me
with trust
viejo corazón puertorriqueño
your feelings cocinan
en mi sangre
el poder de realizarme
and when you whispered
your anger into my ears
when you spoke of
"nosotros los que estamos
preparados con las armas"
it was talk of future
happiness
my ears had not till
that moment heard such
words of promise and of guts
in all of Puerto Rico
old man with the golden chain
and the medallion with an indian

on your chest
I love you
I see in you
what has been
what is coming
and will be
and over your grave
I will write
HERE SLEEPS
A MAN
WHO SEES ALL OF
WHAT EXISTS
AND THAT WHICH WILL EXIST.

Miguel Algarín

Inside Control: my tongue

if the man owns the world
oh white power hidden
behind every word i speak
if the man takes me into his
caverns of meanings in sound
if all my talk is borrowed
from his tongue then i want
hot boiling water to wash
out my mouth i want lye
to soothe my soiled lips
for the english that i
speak betrays my need to be
a self made power

Miguel Algarín

Lolita Lebrón, Recuerdos Te Mandamos

(We send you our love)

From the Nuyorican Poets

FREEEEEE THAT SISTER
FREE THAT LOVING LOVING
LOOOOOVING SISTER
FREE THAT WOMAN   FREE THAT LOVING
LOVING WOMAN
FREE LOLITA LEBRÓN

Sister Sister don't you know a Brother
is not always a Brother
A Brother seems to say Peace and
Power.   Peace and Power.
A Sinner is not always a Sinner
but how could you communicate it
to them,
who understand only hate.
Life seems to say to Lolita Lebrón
Love is stronger than thunder
but Death keeps kissing both of
her cheeks.
In the magnifying glass of the Revolutionary's eyes,
they see the Fox tricked by the
Lions,
and Justice Justice Justice
they seem to call it
but how ugly how dry
is the word Justice
They seem to say
Just us, Just them
I seem to call
Capitalistic Swine.

Lolita Lebrón
Luchastes con el
Sudor y La Verdad
Hermana, Usted tiene que
ver La Claridad
¡Usted ha luchado por La Única
Verdad!

FREEEEEE THAT SISTER
FREE THAT LOVING LOVING LOVING LOVING
SISTER
FREE THAT SISTER, FREE THAT
LOVING LOVING LOVING LOVING SISTER
LOLITA, Te Adoramos
Nos Recordamos
Recuerdos Te Mandamos.

Lucky CienFuegos

IN ORDER TO DESTROY OUR NATION THEY WILL HAVE TO TAKE OUR LIVES

PARA QUITARNOS LA PATRIA TIENEN QUE QUITARNOS LA VIDA

Pedro Albizu Campos

The Book of Genesis According to Saint Miguelito

Before the beginning
God created God
In the beginning
God created the ghettos & slums
and God saw this was good.
So God said,
"Let there be more ghettos & slums"
and there were more ghettos & slums.
But God saw this was plain
so
to decorate it
God created leadbase paint
and then
God commanded the rivers of garbage & filth
to flow gracefully through the ghettos.
On the third day
because on the second day God was out of town
On the third day
God's nose was running
& his jones was coming down and God
in his all knowing wisdom
he knew he was sick
he needed a fix
so God
created the backyards of the ghettos
& the alleys of the slums
& heroin & cocaine
and
with his divine wisdom & grace
God created hepatitis
who begat lockjaw
who begat malaria
who begat degradation
who begat
GENOCIDE
and God knew this was good
in fact God knew things couldn't git better

but he decided to try anyway
On the fourth day
God was riding around Harlem in a gypsy cab
when he created the people
and he created these beings in ethnic proportion
but he saw the people lonely & hungry
and from his eminent rectum
he created a companion for these people
and he called this companion
capitalism
who begat racism
who begat exploitation
who begat male chauvinism
who begat machismo
who begat imperialism
who begat colonialism
who begat wall street
who begat foreign wars
and God knew
and God saw
and God felt this was extra good
and God said
"VAYAAAAAAAA"
On the fifth day
the people kneeled
the people prayed
the people begged
and this manifested itself in a petition
a letter to the editor
to know why? WHY? WHY? que pasa babyyyyyy?
and God said,
"My fellow subjects
let me make one thing perfectly clear
by saying this about that
      NO . . . COMMENT!"
but on the sixth day God spoke to the people
he said . . . "PEOPLE!

the ghettos & the slums
& all the other great things I've created
will have dominion over thee"
and then
he commanded the ghettos & slums
and all the other great things he created
to multiply
and they multiplied
On the seventh day God was tired
so he called in sick
collected his overtime pay
a paid vacation included
But before God got on that t.w.a.
for the sunny beaches of Puerto Rico
He noticed his main man satan
planting the learning trees of consciousness
around his ghetto edens
so God called a news conference
on a state of the heavens address
on a coast to coast national t.v. hook up
and God told the people
to be
COOL
and the people were cool
and the people kept cool
and the people are cool
and the people stay cool
and God said
"Vaya . . . ."

Miguel Piñero

La Metadona Está Cabrona

(Methadone is a bitch)

Constipated-mind castrated-
feelin' frustrated-bein' invaded
by pain
another date el doctor is late
bones ache
got to go downtown underground
no
metadona around
me siento solo y loco socorro
la metadona está cabrona
ain't no snitch methadone is a bitch

but then there's always the wine
when waitin' on line
for the holy water that'll ease your mind
brush aside the concept of time
lo cojo con take it easy

hey my main man there's a new program
they don't care they'll put you on
welfare & feed you that bitter orange
drink you'll swallow from a little plastic
bottle
&
come aboard the metadona train
hey it's so boss better than horse con cocaine
fill a synthetic need
legalize O.D.
can't you see la metadona está cabrona
ain't no snitch methadone is a bitch

what's the difference six days a week you nod out
on the stoop the seventh you nod out on your therapy
group they call you a slob cuz you nod out on the job
and your wood won't throb it just flops . . . flops . . flops . . .

can't yell out ghettocide since you did **abide** & **signed**
on the dotted line
to an agreement of shame who's to blame
but you,
you motherfuckin' lame
oye que lió te buscate mi pana,
tu no sabes que la metadona está cabrona

out on the street you claim to be
a revolutionary
who'll appear on color t.v.
after you git you signal a telephone jingle
& social reentry . . .

you wasn't cool fool
porque yo te ví on t.v.
as you smile & style with your probation
offerin' apolozation for the nation's
programs of computerization genocidation
&
next mention with no hesitation
a manifestation a deadman's declaration
that you were no longer on
DRUGS
but
on
Medication . . . .

Miguel Piñero

No Hay Nada Nuevo en Nueva York

No hay nada nuevo en nueva york
there is nothin' new in new york
te lo digo en inglés
te lo digo en español
la misma situación de opresión
es la única acción en todas
las esquinas de esta nación
un revolver de arrabales que disparán
balas frías contra la policía
la suerte es la muerte que viene
y tiene la misma peste de
pobreza

No hay nada nuevo en nueva york
chico no meta el hocico en welfare
no creas porque la brea es fea
y una maldición que es un bacilón
de la investigación

No hay nada nuevo en nueva york
se solicitan y se necesita
una lluvia de solución
otra obra de revolución—el segundo
movimiento.

No hay nada nuevo en nueva york
jebo trabajar sin dinero en esta
factoria de poesia
para contratar y acabar la estación de esta
gloriosa nación no es un juego
pana creelo hoy y no mañana que
no hay nada nuevo en nueva york.

Miguel Piñero

There Is Nothing New in New York

No hay nada nuevo en nueva york
There is nothing new in new york
I tell you in english
I tell you in spanish
the same situation of oppression
it's the only action in all the corners
of this nation
a revolver ghetto shooting
cold bullets against the police
luck is death which comes and has
the same stench of
poverty

There is nothing new in new york
brother don't stick your nose into welfare
believe me because the tar is ugly
and a curse that's a lot of fun
for the investigators

There is nothing new in new york
we solicit and need
a rain of solution
another work of revolution
a second movement.

There is nothing new in new york
bro work without bread
in this poetry factory
to contract and end the station of
this glorious nation is no game
brotherman believe it today and not tomorrow
that
there is nothing new in new york.

Miguel Piñero

Runnin' Scared

RUNNIN' SCARED—RUNNIN' SCARED
you're goin' nowhere
runnin' with your eyes closed
thinkin' to ease your heavy load

RUNNIN' SCARED
listen to the echos of your shadows
wishin' for easy tomorrows
talkin' into the dead phones of yesterday

RUNNIN' SCARED—RUNNIN' SCARED
you're shifting
you're lifting
you're throwing it all away
it's plainly stamped on the backs of blue jeans
the hopes and hopelessness
of cast-aside dreams
super-star
super-revolutionary
high priest
on neon signs
playin' today
beggin' mom for a dime
runnin' scared
you gettin' nowhere . . .

Compassion—compassion
in burnt bottle caps
tenth of always your last stop
god is the coca-cola bottlin' company
you've heard his voice on NBC
and when he gives it a rest listen to his son on CBS
brought to you live
this ain't no jive
by your friendly neighborhood
soul-buyin' agency
they aim to please
good news ain't guaranteed

ask for mister lucifer
the man with the friendly smile
for your soul he'll walk a mile
no trade in
no deposits
no return
no credit cards accepted . . . but . . .
you can take the layaway plan
with easy pay a mint.

RUNNIN' SCARED—RUNNIN' SCARED
statue of liberty
on 42nd street
lookin' like an old hag
OR
is it a guy in drag
seeeee youuuu laaattteerrrr
got to check out this female impersonator

RUNNIN' SCARED—RUNNIN' SCARED
and you still ain't half way there
can't pick up enough speed
didn't listen to your own decree
now you're stranded on this subway station
called hypocrisy
do you wish to take a runnin' jump?
can't smooth out the lumps
on the high ways
roads and by-ways
and there's a toll booth on this freeway
(freeway?)
an abe or a george
doesn't matter there
ain't no
CHANGE . . . .

Miguel Piñero

A Poem for Joey's Mami's Struggle

On joey's block
102nd street
the atmosphere rains of fear
& hostility & jealousy charms
the nostril hostile when
foreign bodies invade their turf

On the top floor
the fifth floor next door to god
joey's little hermanito & big sister
celebrate their years of pain
their mother's years of strain receive
an ode with miller high life beer
flowin' freely from hand to mouth
& back again
cuz in central park
pasteles y cuchifritos
on the walk
on the run
from the foamin' mouths of
junkies
muggers
outlaws
or just plain ordinary bad guys

she makes that dollar done
but
the evil villain
doesn't prey in the light
all night behind bulbless street lamps
the evil villain
is on the alert lurkin' waitin'
to grab joey's mami's pastele pesos
the evil villain
gets an attitude cuz joey's mami doesn't show
no gratitude for livin' at exploited prices
with welfare lices

On joey's block
the atmosphere rains of fear
& hostility & joey's mami gets it done
she needs the dollar to meet the mornin'
sun . . . .

Miguel Piñero

Seekin' the Cause

he was Dead
he never Lived
died
died
he died seekin' a Cause
seekin' the Cause
because
he said
he never saw the Cause
but
he heard the Cause
heard the cryin' of hungry ghetto children
heard the warnin' from Malcolm
heard tractors pave new routes to new prisons
died seekin' the Cause
seekin' a Cause
he was dead on arrival
he never really Lived
uptown . . . downtown . . . midtown . . . crosstown
body was found all over town
seekin' the Cause
thinkin' the Cause was 75 dollars & gator shoes
thinkin' the cause was sellin' the white lady to black
children
thinkin' the cause is to be found in gypsy rose or j.b.
or dealin' wacky weed
and singin' du-wops in the park after some chi-chiba
he died seekin' the Cause
died seekin' a Cause

and the Cause was dyin' seekin' him
and the Cause was dyin' seekin' him
and the Cause was dyin' seekin' him
he wanted a color t.v.
wanted a silk on silk suit
he wanted the Cause to come up like the mets & take the
world series

73

he wanted . . . he wanted . . . he wanted . . . he wanted to want more
wants but
he never gave
he never gave
he never gave his love to children
he never gave his heart to old people
&
never did he ever give his soul to his people
he never gave his soul to his people
because he was busy seekin' a Cause
busy
busy perfectin' his voice to harmonize the national anthem
with spiro t agnew
busy perfectin' his jive talk so that his flunkiness
doesn't show
busy perfectin' his viva-la-policía speech
downtown . . . uptown . . . midtown . . . crosstown
his body was found all over town
seekin' a Cause
seekin' the Cause
found
in the potter fields of an o.d.
found
in the bowery with the dt's

his legs were left in viet-nam
his arms were found in sing-sing
his scalp was on nixon's belt
his blood painted the streets of the ghetto
his eyes were still lookin' for jesus to come down on
some cloud & make everythin' all right
when jesus died in attica
his brains plastered all around the frames of the pentagon
his voice still yellin' stars & stripes 4 ever
riddled with the police bullets his taxes bought
he died seekin' a Cause
seekin' the Cause

while the Cause was dyin' seekin' him
he died yesterday
he's dyin' today
he's dead tomorrow
died seekin' a Cause
died seekin' the Cause
& the Cause was in front of him
& the Cause was in his skin
& the Cause was in his speech
& the Cause was in his blood
but
he died seekin' the Cause
he died seekin' a Cause
he died
deaf
dumb
&
blind
he died
died
 & never found his Cause
because
you see he never never
knew that he was the
Cause

Miguel Piñero

Message of My People

Wake up tomorrow mornin' a Boricua
'N' listen to the futile sound of poverty
Divided 'n' afraid by stomach growls that envy
The shine of a car before the odor of baked bread
'N' a child who breakfasts plaster
While a junky seeks the paradox of a cure

Wake up tomorrow mornin' a Boricua
'N' walk to a store with no money, no food stamps
Only to find a grocer who doesn't understand spanish
But who understands you well on the 1st 'n' 16th
'N' not wanting to come back empty-handed
You keep walking towards more defeat
'N' a final end of: "Yes, I'll fuck with you"

Wake up tomorrow mornin' a Boricua
'N' prepare to work in a factory
Which you hate the piss-stain smell of
'N' every day you come back with callous-hands
Only to find a son in need of a fix
A daughter with bleach-blond hair
A wife cooking the leftovers of yesterday
'N' not being able to cry for a man is not supposed to cry
Under this system

Wake up tomorrow mornin' a Boricua
'N' feel the chills of a July mornin'
Moving your every pore to grab the 007
While your wife cries: "No! You can kick!"
You fall to your knees with nose running sweating 'n' unemotional tear
'N' your son who pats you on your head 'n' says:
"What's wrong papi, are you sick?"

Wake up tomorrow mornin' a Boricua
'N' walk the streets with a new dress
Hoping no one finds out it's from Orchard St.
While you hold on to the extra $5 for a bag of reefer
Which you don't dig but been told it's hip
By a bunch of gringo-orientated motherfuckers
Who think of love through an erection of their penis

Wake up tomorrow mornin' a Boricua
Wake up tomorrow mornin' a Boricua
'N' you will know that Borinqueño is a state of love for our people
A state of tranquil beauty for our Land
We are being denied this
This is why Borinqueño is a state of REVOLUTION

BORICUA REVOLUTION!!

T. C. Garcia

Situation Heavy

Situation, heavy!
Situation, the democracy!
Situation, heavy!
Situation, the heck with the democracy!

Intellectual, Congressional fools,
Why, you don't even know how to use your
own earthly tools.
They stand there and send rockets to the stars
while there's people here on earth saying,
Hey, I'm starved!
They sit on their throne and beat their wood
and have the audacity to say, we're not understood.

Understood! Look at the nation you've created.
Toy boys that are told men don't cry,
they're only there to scare away flies,
to fight and die.

OOOOOH, FUNKY HONKY!

Your creation, my sacrification,
Your creation, my destination.
Situation, heavy!
Situation, the heck with the democracy!

You say today is responsible for yesterday.
Well, it is.
Today is responsible for yesterday.
For you created today!
You created yesterday!
And you're creating the sorrows of tomorrow!
And if people are not for you, but against you,

you push your dope and tell the people to have hope.
Hope in what?
To do what for you?
Sing what type of blues?
Situation, heavy!

Thank you, thank you! Thank you for your schools.
For you taught me how to eat with your silverware.
You taught me how to comb my lovely hair.
You taught me how to create my own tools.
Thank you for your schools.
You taught me how to manipulate the so-called great
and how to have a good debate.
And I'll keep next to you by going to your schools.
I'll keep going to your schools, you dumb fools.

Angel Berrocales

The Teacher of Life

Man 1: Hey, look at me! I'm really what I want to be.
I'm a big part of the society.
Hey, look at me! For I'm only thirty-three.
I got my apartment in the Avenue of Fermenting
and my parents gave me a limousine.
Hey, look at me! But don't talk to me, please
don't talk to me. For I'm only thirty-three.
I have all the money but I don't know what to say
and to know what to say, I would pay.
Teach me, it's not hard for me to learn. I was in
school for twenty-eight years. But what good is it
doing me if I'm still a little boy full of fears?
Please look at me. I want to be noticed, I want to
be focused.
Man 2: I am the teacher. I teach all grades in elementary
school. For in order to teach a child properly you
must teach him when he's real young. And if you're a teacher
like me, he'll grow up to a real dumb-dumb.
We made history books. And the only reason history
doesn't say the truth all the time is because it will
make us look bad most of the time.
But we sure enough made history books.
We must keep the young children dumb for we don't
want a black president.
I can see it all now: black-eyed peas for breakfast,
chitlins for snacks, grits for lunch, and watermelons
for dinner.
NO: It's got to be the way it is now.
We made the country.
For we're the society.
The one and only Society.

Angel Berrocales

A day when clinkers, sparrows and canaries jitterbugged down the street with a latin accent

sat in the park / on a hundred-six street
between west end ave. & broadway
the sun opened its zipper / peed over
tenements / reading victor hernandez /
cruise down river / opened my eyes /
to see sawdust / coming through

intellectual eight year olds / create
vietnams / over ground balls / violence that's
all they think of / had diarrhea in wall-less
run-down bathrooms / abandoned by anglo-saxon
landlords / coming in different colors

cold breeze starts humming / two hamburgers
that brought the fire hydrants / to take away the
remains of natural america / the grass and the baby pine
trees locked in a cage / with the door already closed
on buffy sainte-marie / beware this street patrolled by
uniform guards

was condensed enough / to be evaporated in
containers / to be sold in a&p food stores /
with strange eyes beaming at still drawings /
that come to life in midnight hours / looking
for a new trick / to hang out in west end bars
of solitude / to deposit litter on the floors
of empty apartments

floating on rockaway waves / in midtown
office congestions / the sky became clear /
with mucus on the lips of colonial imposition /
y un negrito committed suicide / choking
with paranoia.

Americo Casiano

A Junkie's Heaven

His sacrifice was not in vain
though he died because of an abscessed
brain
a junkie dreamt
of his lament
When I die
I shall go to a land
where the cocaine is clean
and I'll smoke my pot only when it's
at the darkest of green
here all the angels are junkies
and the Christ is so hip
that for the crime of my bootlegged
wine
he'll demand two sips
yes, come to my heaven where all
the junkies walk free . . . and
remember all you potheads out
there
the smoke is on me . . . .

Shorty Bón Bón

Puerto Rico's Reply

Roll around in a VW around
the beautiful beaches of Puerto Rico
smiling Burger Kings and McDonald's
heading to Gurabo my hometown
we stopped for a while and kept
moving around we're going
up a hill Miguel is puzzled
his mind seems to wander out to
the streets he is
checking the beat he's
thundering inside glitter in his eye
stop the car don't go no more
I want to see if there is
any Puerto Rican out here
in beautiful Puerto Rico
we get ready to watch Miguel
get hit in the eye we grab the pipe
Miguel stepped out he stopped a
man then quietlike and scared
he said to the man "are there any Puerto
Ricans in Puerto Rico?" we got ready
for static the man replied
Miguel came back surprised
we asked him what he
replied Miguel said
"I don't know I don't know
I don't think so."

Dadi Piñero

84

Life Now

UNDERSTAND
THAT THIS
IS NOW
AND THAT WAS BEFORE
NOW IS NOW
BEFORE WAS BEFORE
WHAT HAPPENED HAPPENED
AND WHAT'S STARTING NOW
IS BEGINNING AND WHAT'S PAST
HAS ENDED AND WHAT'S AHEAD OF US
WILL BE THE END

Dadi Piñero

PART II

EVOLUTIONARY POETRY

The evolutionary section of the anthology is made up of the poetry that tells the story of people who are looking out at the system and trying to deal with it. There are many poems of anger but the thrust of these poems is to move out and try to direct the bureaucracy. These are the tales of the struggle of "adjusting" the outside to the inside. Roberto Nazario once wrote to a city official who arrogantly announced that his agency was taking over the management of buildings from community people. Nazario wrote that:

> Our great city is going bankrupt. Pass
> the word along Mr. that we are going to
> bang on your doors, day after day, month
> after month, until you all agree that we
> have something to contribute to the City
> of New York as citizens of this great
> City. This is what New York City people
> want now, not next year or the year after.

Bimbo Rivas' simple request for a job to save him from despair and self-disdain moves the reader through the birth pains of adjusting,

> A Job
> A simple job
> A place to meet the day head on
> with force and vigor.

It is a strong and strengthening attitude that Bimbo takes. He knows that mental health means work,

> A Job my brain to put to work
> My brain that tells me I'm OK.

It is an attitude of self-help that pervades: for example,

Adopt-a-Building, Sweat Equity, and El Teatro Ambulante are some of the organic centers that have been uniting people and employing their time in work that rewards them with housing, building skills, and theater.

T. C. Garcia feels the need to grow into strength but he is apprehensive. He suspects that we are not really ready, that we are not to be trusted with weapons for self-protection,

> But . . . We have to grow . . .
>   'cause we cannot—
>   we must not!—
> put M16's 'n' AK47's
> in the hands of Brothers 'n' Sisters
> whose political scope can't see further than "jitterbugging"
>
> We have to grow . . .
> to take it.
> We have to grow . . .
> to take it.
> We have to grow . . .
> to learn how to take it.

The speaker of this poem wants to fight but he is afraid to depend on those "whose political scope" is not ready for the struggle and the "perpetual change— / on which the creation of every nation is founded." The speaker of T. C. Garcia's poems has the deep conviction that continuous change is the one inviolable law of man, yet the speaker is not always trustful of the change.

Jesús Papoleto Meléndez's poem "sister, para nuestras hermanas" (for our sisters) tells the story of the revolutionary woman whose ideals are betrayed by a man who wants "to lay her" more than he wants to struggle along with her:

> have you seen the revolutionary sister
> rappin' to the masses of poor /
>   she talks about revolution /   change
>   she talks about redistributing wealth
>   to all
>
> she's read Mao   & Marx   Che & Lenin . . .

But the truth of Papoleto's poem is that the "you" has not "seen" her. What we learn of the "you" in the poem is that he does not understand that "she" is searching to "adjust" the outside to her needs and his needs and the needs of her children. Instead, she is seen as a sexual object.

Americo Casiano gets close to the cutting edge of the betrayal of the woman in our society when he says,

> and can you remember
> the last time you saw mami smile?
>
> an old friend greeted her one day,
> told her how good of a woman she was,
> for raising such a fine family
> and she smiled.
>
> the old man didn't know
> she sacrificed her life
> for it to happen.
> sixteen years for it to happen
> sixteen years, sixteen long years
> working in the garment district
> all to see it happen.

There is no sparing it, there is no softening of it, mami suffers and she is not given recognition. Americo's poem is the lyrical highlight of this section. The flow of emotions is spare, clear, tough and honest. The poem drives its story of pain and despair right into the subneurological sentiments of the reader until, by the end of the poem, the reader feels anxiously protective about "mami":

> you say you saw her smile the other day
> even though pops beat her up
> with a bat
> after that he went to see his other woman.

Mami's evolution has taken her through much despair but the purity of her devotion binds and keeps the worlds of her children together. She is still the central point of reference.

Miguel Algarín

91

A Job

A Job
to feed the time I spend adrift
in search for substance in the street
Awake at three a.m.
not knowing where or when the end
will come to my disdain
A Job
A simple job
A place to meet the day head on
with force and vigor
with fervor bigger than a winning independence slate
A Job
A Job my brain to put to work
My brain that tells me I'm OK
My brain that can produce the necessary rhythm
to set my idle body straight
My brain that yearns for a sincere break
I don't expect the world to stop for me
To stop its mission for my sake
I only ask for a clearer path
to put my brains and hands to work
to prove my worth
A Job
A Job my God
A Job that's better than the street
its hustle
and its pests
A Job
A Job that also fills my heart
not just my belly as does the city welfare
check
A Job with all the benefits
correlated with the sweat and time
invested by myself
A Job that don't step on my pride
A Job that don't shorten my life on earth
that will inspire me to help my bosses

their part of the proceeds collect
I need a JOB to keep my peace with God
A Job to make me stop wishing for an early grave
A Job
A Job
I NEED A JOB TODAY
Folks that got a job
a job that does its job
can see some sense in this relate
folk that lost their faith
that rot away with pain
DAY AFTER DAY
Strike at each other
hoping to find
in greater pain
a sedative
it's all too relative
my friends
A man without a JOB
is lost in the labyrinth of
HELL.

Bimbo

Biological

Puerto Rican
children
have nothing to
say in school.
Pedro said the
other day "I've
got the D train
running up my
leg and the F train
in my crotch."
The teacher gave
him a demerit
and said "Sit
down." He sat and
peed all down
his pants. The
teacher sent him
to the principal
for incorrigible
behavior. Pedro
knew he had not
been understood.
Puerto Rican
children
have nothing to
say in school.

Miguel Algarín

Posed Release

Turquoise blue
Smacks my eye
Tomato red
Pinches my tongue
Apple green-leaf
Soft arouser
Light afternoon
Made particular
Through rays
That congeal
Shifting green into
Some liveable
Reality, —
It is time for
Green to be all green
Ultimate arrangement
Of self into,
And snugly,
Soothing meanings of
Blue dances in green
Devouring afternoons

Miguel Algarín

Tangiers

Down to the Kasba with me,
Mikey, Dadi and Lucky
down to the Kasba with us
right into the hollering poverty
of Tangiers where boys sell
themselves for little more than
a dollar's caress, where people
are hungry, go hungry and
will remain under attack
from stomach cramps
and muscle spasms caused
by rampant malnutrition
Tangiers yo ya te quiero
estoy enamorado d'être ici
dans le nord d'Afrique
dans la ville la plus belle
que j'avais jamais vue—Tangiers
I love the happy tyranny of being
attacked on all sides for my
American connection "les dollars,"
the green mercurochrome that heals
all the scabby wounds of pennilessness
and homelessness and hunger
Tangiers your children are les
plus beaux du monde and yet
they scurry down your gutter-alleys
bleeding hopelessness
Tangiers your bleeding children speak
three, four, five languages before
they're five years old—your streets
create maximum survival pressure
making your children's tongues
control alternate systems of speech
as they hustle the cracks of the streets
and the queens from the continent—
four spanish queens glide into
the Café Central like Columbus's

97

ships must have slid into the new
world: grace, poise, perfume, vaseline
and an uncontrollable gleam in their eyes
as the boys parade themselves—
the older queen exhibits a skin as
wrinkled as Lady Wishfort's cracked
and peeling face
the other orders mint tea with little sugar
as his eyes anxiously rape a twelve
year old crotch, the boy smiles, a ten dirham
bill is flashed and a new romance has just
been bought, the other two devour every
young box that comes into sight and the
boys parade as the ladies' anxious helmet
jones keep coming down
beautiful boys approach
beautiful boys go away
beautiful boys approach
beautiful boys go away
all are for sale
ten dirhams for this one
twenty dirhams for the other
Tangiers is Forty-Second Street
morality with an Orchard Street
sales pitch—un muchachito
tuerto approaches, he tries us
out in french, italian, german
then english
he hit the jackpot, our ears betray
us, he knows we've understood him
now comes the onrush,
the insistence, the pleading,
the assault, the guilt trip
tripping us up sending our
hands into our pockets searching
for a dirham to leave our consciousness
clean, to buy us freedom from

the boy's imploring hustle
we are hand to mouth Nuyoricans
suddenly made rich by greater poverty
than our own
but wait!
Tangiers, our inner-city jungles
match yours and they are equally
poor, dirty, misunderstood, desperate
and we are struggling, hustling men
just like your boys
but we exist inside the belly of the
monster, we are the pistons that
move the roughage through Uncle
Sam's intestines, we keep the flow
of New York happening
we are its muscles
and its castor oil
we are its poets, its historians,
its dishwashers, its toilet cleaners,
and its revolutionaries:
a revolutionary is un merchand ambulant,
a revolutionary is a petit taxi
carrying truth as its fare,
a revolutionary breathes through his mouth
while all others breathe through their
nose and in his throat he separates
the oxygen from the waste before
air reaches his lungs—
le Café Central at the Petit Chico
stays open 24 hours a day
and once again Miky and I
are at the pure heart
        the vibrating pulse
of Tangiers—people are drawn
around the square
like moscas to flypaper,
coffee, mint tea, toast, butter and

jelly no beer no alcohol no wine
only café crême, talk and endless
begging—many blind men
        many maimed men
        many starving cats
        and hungry young boys
as I drink café crême, talk and give
dirhams when I'm moved to share
my short change,
I am reminded of the
        Stratégies de l'économie
of Europe and I'm struck by the fact
that:
        Les "managers" sont les
        moteurs de l'économie
        L'age des masses a besoin
        de propulseurs qui sachent faire
        mouvoir les gens et les
        choses. Et le verbe anglais
        "to manage" ne signifie au
        fond rien d'autre. Toutefois,
        l'activité que couvre ce vocable ne
        provient pas d'Angleterre ou
        d'Amérique, mais d'Allemagne
England gave its language
America invented abstract management
now Germany takes it to heart and creates
les plus importantes écoles de
cadres dirigéants privée dans le monde,
Dictator Spinola resigns in Portugal
while Miky, Lucky and I are
ready to become the managing
directors of the streets of Tangiers—
our first down to the money for food
trip happens with Toni,
Toni is making his économie
balance on the sale of our 1968

Ford Transit Van, our home for
sale in Tangiers streets, our
papers are not in legal order,
our first buyer offers two hundred
fifty no more and be happy
you've got an offer
we decide not to sell Margarita-Tanya
we're hundreds of dollars
short of what we've planned
but I wouldn't sell for two fifty
since I didn't like getting pinned
by a slickster from the streets
of Tangiers where the rich live
and the very poor are the indicators
whereby a man can know he's rich
      well anyway
Toni and his buddy poured fear
into the atmosphere because of our
irregular papers proving ownership
of le voiture, we listened with respect
but we left before eating with him,
we began to move our bed and
all our blankets back into the van and as
we reassembled our little moving
fortress we realized we were back
into our womb, our internal place
of private control which keeps us
all responsible for our moving on
our own—

LA ÚNICA DIFERENCIA ENTRE
UN ARABE Y UN NUYORICAN
ES LA MANERA EN QUE SOPLA EL VIENTO

THE ONLY DIFFERENCE BETWEEN
AN ARAB AND A PUERTO RICAN
IS THE WAY IN WHICH THE WIND
BLOWS

Miguel Algarín

101

Teatro

Teatro
a street scene
a scene of
us, you and me
a scene
a Puerto Rican scene
The scene of
us
as in we
as we express us
and touch the hearts
when we
release our inner feelings
of
I am me and you are you
Teatro
as in you
as in we
of
THE LOWER EAST SIDE
that set aside
that higher side
down to us
when we go up
and look down to them
Teatro
a freedom of life
as in reality to us
for function of we

as in Ambulante
Teatro
a scene
as in
feeling of feel
of
expression of you
to us
of
OH SHIT
WOW
Y ESTÁ
PERO BIEN HEAVY DUTY MAN!!
sí
a street scene
a feeling of love
for our people
as in us
that are we
of Ambulante

Martita Morales

Así Era Yo

Así era yo
aprovechaba las tardes
y en mis manos
sujetaba para compartir

como ese muchachito
para pasear
algunas frutas
con mis hermanitos
de ayer, de hoy, y de mañana

Hermanitos de recuerdos
hermanitos que todavía duermen

en el suelo de mi borinquen

desde que mi padre murió
dejamos aquel sol

La vida está un poco cambiada

que era símbolo de nuestras tierras

nuestra mañana y nuestro
sacrificio

en el monte quedo
dejando mi alma destrosada

hoy miro en el espejo
con las lágrimas asomadas
y a la niña de mis ojos
y en mi mente se desfilan . . .

. . . AQUELLOS GOLPES
de mi viejo

que me enseñaron a ser hombre
y a conocer el enojo
y a desafiar a todo
lo que se interponía

en mi camino.

Carlos Conde

That's How I was

That's how I was
I took advantage of the
afternoons
and in my hands
to share with

brothers of memory
brothers that still sleep

since my father died
we left that sun
our morning and our
sacrifice

today I look in the mirror
with tears showing
and on the pupils of my eyes
and in my mind parade . . .

that taught me to be a man
and to know anger
and to confront everything
that I know he put there

Carlos Conde
(translation of Miguel Algarín)

like that child

to walk
some fruits
my little brothers
of yesterday, today, tomorrow

      —on Borinquen's soil

Life is a little changed
that was the symbol of our land

were left in the mountains
leaving my soul destroyed

. . . THOSE BEATINGS
from my old man

in my path

puerto rican graffiti

sit in my '57 Cadillac
with your john's bargain store blouse,
bubblegum sticking to your frizzies,
and bare feet smelling of bacalao.
little anthony and tito puente sing
through black sweat—
aquí viene the coquito man
aquí viene superman
who does the cha-cha-cha
and lives in the white house.
broken bottles in the street
shine like diamonds at our feet.
beer smells wine smells rum smells
cover the night like lace
at a first communion.
an imported tropical breeze
goes up your nose disguised
as a sudden whiff of florida water,
a giant cockroach is saying his bedtime rosaries
but los jibaros de la calle
keep on hanging out
of a four-door metal space ship
temporarily grounded on e. 112 st.
ready to take off any minute
to become
the first spics on the moon.

Amina Muñoz

149th St. winter

it was a cold afternoon
possessed by the innumerable
faceless devils in charge of hell.
shango and yemayá
the dispossessed gods
of the neighborhood
were dressed in gray,
their colorful attire
in cold storage as a protest.
they will not be loud and tribal again.
tarzan will have no background music
for a while. not until the sun rises
in sun-kissed faces again.

Amina Muñoz

"welcome to san juan, oldest city in the u.s."

1.
shag by paul mcgregor's
heartburn by mcdonald's
a cuchifrito face
smiles, oblivious
to the facts of death the
promises of a better life
tried to camouflage.

come to paradise,
they said—
let us fly you,
our puerto rico—
let us get drunk
with bacardi and don Q
and the blood of those
who dare say no.

the sun
it is very hot,
is very hot
in the cane fields—
makes you crawl
on your knees—
is this what they meant
by stoop labor?

2.
on TV the politician smiles
an ultrabrite smile, saying
you've come a long way baby—
unemployment has risen from 15% to 25%.
three families
that live in the same house
watch him, amazed.
TV has become very popular here.
the beach has a sign—
KEEP OFF—

U.S. PROPERTY it says.
spineless nondefinitions
of identityless mediocrity
try to convince everyone, including themselves,
that they are the new conquistadores.
white suit arrogance
cuff link authority
and illusions of control
that can't control
their own bad breath.

3.
meanwhile a young student
at rio piedras lies on her concrete grave.
the national guard decided
she got in the way
of the 51st star of the yanqui flag.

puerto rico chafes under a sign
KEEP OFF—
U.S. PROPERTY
it says.

(Para la memoría de la querida compañera, Antonia Martinez.
Nuestra lucha vencerá, Antonia.)

Amina Muñoz

a chant

it's on the roof
100 proof
plátanos
bacalao
and a million african gods
bump their way up madison ave.
to 116 st.
cause
it's in my sneaker
a bag of reefer and
willie colon knows
the dominoes
on the table
merengue to
ave maría and la plena
and when they party
they drink bacardi—
cause puerto ricans are bad
uh-huh
puerto ricans are bad
uh-huh.

Amina Muñoz

sister,
para nuestras hermanas
(sister
for our sisters)

have you seen the revolutionary sister
rappin' to the masses of poor /
        she talks about revolution /   change
        she talks about redistributing wealth
        to all

she's read Mao   & Marx   Che & Lenin
she's true /   for real
she believes in what she does
she loves /
        she loves you /
        she loves her people.
she sleeps little /   works hard
sometimes her eyes show it
she tries to hide it /   she smiles
she's friendly /   loves children
she talks with junkies
& understands
        she's pretty /   beautiful shape
            she's a woman
& she loves.
she'll die /   loving
loving you.
        / i understand you want to lay her.

Jesús Papoleto Meléndez

Puerto Rican Epitaph

NEED
need . . .
I NEED . . . YOU NEED
PEOPLE KEEP RAPPING ABOUT WHAT THEY NEED /
They lie, steal, FUCK TO GET WHAT THEY NEED /
MARIO NEEDS A NEW TIRE FOR HIS GRAND PRIX /
ELENA NEEDS A NEW DRESS TO RIDE IN MARIO'S NEW CAR
CARLOS NEEDS TO FUCK ELENA /
ELENA NEEDS CARLOS TO BUY HER THE NEW DRESS SHE
    NEEDS /
MARIO NEEDS CARLOS' LOOKS TO GET ELENA /
CARLOS NEEDS TO ROB TO GET ELENA THE NEW DRESS /
ELENA NEEDS TO PLAY ON CARLOS FOR THE NEW DRESS /
MARIO NEEDS TO BORROW FOR A NEW TIRE TO RIDE ELENA
    AROUN' /
MARIO ELENA 'N' CARLOS NEED /
THEY ALL NEED . . . WE ALL NEED /
MARIO NEEDS TO DIE IN BIG CAR ACCIDENT LIKE PAUL
    NEWMAN /
ELENA NEEDS BLOND WIG TO WALK AROUND' 42nd street /
CARLOS NEEDS TO GET A FIX 'CAUSE HE COULDN'T GET
    ELENA /
NEED . . . NEED
THEY ALL NEED /
I NEED . . . YOU NEED . . . WE NEED /
MARIO . . . ELENA . . . 'N' CARLOS NEED /
THEY ALL NEED THEMSELVES
BUT CAN'T SEE FURTHER THAN DRESSES CARS 'N' A
GOOD FUCK /
THEY CAN'T SEE THEY'RE A DYING RACE /
A DYING RACE FOR SEEING WHITE NEEDS—NOT PUERTO
    RICAN NEEDS /
THEY NEED RICE 'n' BEANS—BUT NOT CHULETA Y POLLO /
THEY CAN'T SEE . . .

    THEY'RE BLIND—BLIND—BLIND /
    —BLINDED TO WHAT'S HAPPENING IN PUERTO RICO
    —BLINDED BY FANCY HOTELS 'N' SUNNY BEACHES
    —BLINDED BY TWA's "YO HABLO ESPAÑOL" /
    BLIND . . .

NEVER SEEING
NEVER SEEING LA HAMBRE DEL BARRIO
WAITING AT FOUR IN THE MORNING
TO ROB VESINA'S TOÑITA'S MILK 'N'
JUANITA'S TOO—
SO THAT MAMA WILL HAVE SOME FOR THE OTHERS /
YES—THEY NEED TO SEE THIS /
BUT THEY HAVE OTHER NEEDS:
THEY NEED THIS . . . THEY NEED THAT—
THEY NEED TO BUY AT FLORSHEIM
SHOES NEVER NEEDED BEFORE—
THEY NEED TO BUY AT TIFFANY'S . . .
OR NEED JUST TO BE AROUN' THE PLACE (no ticket, no laundry)—
THEY NEED TO SEE BIG WHITE PSYCHIATRIST
WHO TELLS THEM THEY NEED MORE HELP—
THEY NEED TO SEE BIG FANCY PLAYS
'N' NEED NOT UNDERSTAND THEM /
THEY NEED THIS . . .
THEY NEED THAT . . .
(OOOHH PAPI, PAPI—I NEED IT—I DON'T WANT IT—I NEED
    IT)

MARIO—ELENA—CARLOS—PUERTO RICANS—
BORICUAS . . . PORTORROS . . . JIBARAS . . . JIBAROS—
REVOLUTIONARIES OF PUERTO RICO NEED /
NEED! NEED! NEED! THEY NEED TO FUCK A WHITE WOMAN
TO SEE IF IT RUBS OFF /
THEY NEED TO WEAR FANCY CUBAN CHAINS
NOT REALIZING IT'S A BY-PRODUCT OF THE BIG WHITE
    CHAIN /
THEY NEED THE COP-MAN . . . THEY NEED THE BOLITA-MAN
THEY NEED A GOOD PRESIDENT OF THE UNITED STATES
    OF AMERIKA /
THEY NEED TO PRAY ON SUNDAYS—'N' PRAY 'N' PRAY 'N'
    PRAY

(OOOHH THEY NEED TO PRAY THE WHITE BOOGY MAN WON'T
    THROW
THEM OFF THEIR RAT-INFESTED HOMES)

115

THEY NEED! THEY NEED!
THEY WAS BORN NEEDIN'
THEY WILL DIE NEEDIN'
THEY WAS BORN TO DIE NEEDIN'
BY A VALUE SYSTEM WHO SAYS
"PUERTO RICAN—YOU NEED AMERIKA—YOU HEAR."
AND BEING KOOL PUERTO RICAN—
THEY STAYED KOOL PUERTO RICAN—BY NEEDIN'/
THEY DON'T KNOW—THEY NEED TO KNOW!—WE NEED TO
    KNOW—
THAT

    PEOPLE'S ONLY NEED
    IS TO REVOLT / . . .

        'CAUSE NO MAN, NO (G) gOD
        NEEDS NOTHING . . . BUT
        TO CHANGE WHAT <u>NEEDS</u>   TO BE CHANGED!

T. C. Garcia

When was the last time you saw mami smile?

when was the last time
you saw mami smile?

i mean really smile,
just for nothing smile,
peace of mind smile,
humble smile.
can you remember?
i know i can't.

i remember her smiling
because you ridiculed her
in front of your friends
and she smiled cause
it was the thing to do.

            / you thought it was cute
            but inside she felt hurt,
            ashamed, stupid.

and can you remember,
the last time mami smiled?

an old friend greeted her one day,
told her how good of a woman she was,
for raising such a fine family
and she smiled.

the old man didn't know
she sacrificed her life
for it to happen.
sixteen years for it to happen.
sixteen years, sixteen long years
working in the garment district,
all to see it happen.

to see her daughters become putas y tecatas
on simpson street and southern boulevard,
putas on university levels to americanized dreams
and her sons strung out on the holy bible
and themselves
                    / ooow i'm bad
                    got my rainbow colored playboys
                    got my long layered haircut. . . .
                    maybe next week i'll turn it into an afro
                    naw brother . . . have you seen esos niggers lately
                    wearing esos braids
                    look like farina and buckwheat of the little
                    rascals.

and when was the last time you saw mami smile?

i mean really smile,
just for nothing smile,
peace of mind smile,
humble smile.

you say you saw her smile the other day
                    even though pops beat her up
                    with a bat . . .
                    after that he went to see his other woman.

there were three little boys running upstairs
after three little girls
and mami smiled
                    for she knew,
                    what it would lead to. . . .
                    it happened to her.

paca sits on the third avenue el
with her legs open
and mami just smiles,
painfully.

you say you love to see mami smile
but really smile . . .
like when her grandchildren call her . . .
                    abuela, abuela, abuela
in the middle of the night
because el cuco is after them.

hey but look,
she's smiling now
and i'll never make her feel bad again.
i'll always bring you flowers
to keep you smiling
and i'll see you every day,
keep your place clean
and, and, an . . .

"sorry son but we have to close the coffin"

pity i never had a chance to tell her,
te adoro madre mía. . . .

Americo Casiano

Twice a Month Is Mother's Day

Waitin' for the mailman to come—early in the mornin'
'fore the junkies wake—twice a month—the 16th & the 1st—
stoop draped with people hungry eyed—&
winos dying of thirst—Mama pushed back the walls of my room
hurriedly i dress—removin' dead roaches from the coffee cup
bury 'em navy style—down the kitchen sink—
with a quick eulogy spiced with puerto rican profanity

II

Again our roommate who lives rent free & eats better than me—
has successfully 'voided the snare—& takes the prize—
Mama thinks she'll use cyanide—i don't think it makes a
difference to him or her—& don't think it works either—
If lead-paint-chippin' plaster won't kill him—i think
nothin' will—Why not consider him part of the family—
like the beautifullll white people on t.v. do with their
dog & cat only difference is our pet will be a rat

III

hate coffee con powdered leche—surplus—all gone—no money too . . .

IV

Sold the cheese to don florencio el bodeguero—for two containers
of milk—today he'll sell it back . . .
doña carmen—doña adelina—comai toñita—hurry corran he comin'
el caltero—nes builin' down—don luis hurry or the tecatos will
get your check—don luis is very old & he scared of los perdidos—
how are you ladies today—everyone says—tan ju bien—an ju—ho arl ju
don't like his smile—don't like the way he says ladies
don't like the way he says it's mother's day. . . .

V

On the first—got a paper bag did number two in it—was goin' to
drop it on his bald head—as he takes off his hat & bows to the
comadres on the stoop—after he says it's mother's day—
Mama caught me—held me—held the bag till he went away—she smells it—
she looks inside—she screams—out the window it went—more screams—
with curses too—Mama still screamin' at me—yellin' she gonna
hit me—NO she holds my arms—WHY? ¿PORQUÉ? cuz i don't like the
way he says it's mother's day . . .
she laughs—outside they curse—Mama starts laughin' stops laughin'

123

now she'll hit me—No she starts cryin'—kissin my head—
don't like seein' mama cry . . .

VI

Everyone is cryin'—they all want to change the thing with Mama
but i am the oldest i will go—protect her from . . .
like the day the big guy took Mama's purse on delancey st.
i ran behind parked cars—hidin'—he stops—i snatch it from him—
ran back—was a real hero—just like john wayne . . .

VII

Mama looks real pretty today—even doña olga looks pretty—Mama says
"have to change el checke before the collectors come around—"
doña rosa y doña maría didn't get the checke today—doña maría
she says she take the nenes to the wilfredo oficina let 'em feed 'em
everyone says sí-sí-sí-sí-sí Y que más—cuz they know she comes back
for them—Mama says she will speak for her tomorrow at the center
Mama she speaks very good english . . .

VIII

oh-oh-oh here come the tecatos —los perdidos—los motos—they will
stand there on the corner with their arms around their bellies
lookin' lookin' until . . .

IX

AHAHAHAHaaa here comes doña rosa she is pretty—NO she is
        beauuttiiiffuulllll
NO she is prettier than "pretty please with sugar on top" . . . wow
she says the investigator came around last night & almost caught
don miguel—who is the nenés tío—everyone says sí-sí-sí-sí Y que más—
didn't find don miguel—pero—he found his shoes—everyone says sí-sí-sí
Y que más she says they belong to her son rikie—he says tooooo biiiggg
everyone says sí-sí-sí-sí Y que mas—she says he now wants to sleep with
her or he'll never give back her checke & this time for good—everyone
says sí-sí-sí-sí Y que mas—she says que se va hacer
when me & Mama are leavin' i ask doña rosa why the investigator wants
to sleep with her—coño I don't even like sleepin' with my two
hermanos—everyone was feelin' good cuz they all start laughin'

X

But everyone is always happy on the 1st & on the 16th no other
days—people are always sad . . . but not today—not today—
TODAY THE WHOLE WORLD IS CHANGIN' THEIR WELFARE
        CHECK . . .

Miguel Piñero   124

Love Story

2 typewriters were making out with each other, it was far out,
every time one of the typewriters came the bell would go off
and all the keys would fall back into the wrong place and you
could see the expression of satisfaction on the type ribbon,
how did they meet? only the two typewriters know for sure and
so far it looks like they are not giving out that information,
the affair was an affair that was more than an affair as far
as the 2 typewriters were concerned, one was not playing up to
the other one, it was beyond reality what they had going on,
it was not a mixed couple, an electric typewriter and a manual,
they were both manual typewriters from the same pawnshop,
I think this is the reason why they got along so flawlessly,
they were so into each other typing paper was not necessary

Pedro Pietri

PART III

DUSMIC POETRY

"Dusmic" is a new word. It defines the process of transforming aggression being directed at you by another person (or, more generally, society) into your strength.

Luz Marina Rodriguez knows that the politics of love leaves women converting negative energy into positive feelings. Luz once told Vilma Linares, an actress in the Nuyorican Theater Festival, that whenever her father showed no love she had to be patient and show him love. That's how Luz's mother taught her to absorb aggression and transform it into strength:

> i feel the eve
> of my body
> flowing through
> the cycle of woman.
> blood rush down
> cleanse my womb.
> my hair at motion,
> limbs in stimulation,
> effecting sensation,
> submerging in love.

Because the poet knows there is no safety and knows that he exists in chaos he has to pull himself together while twirling. Pedro Pietri's poem "do not let" creates a space where the reader experiences objects melting into each other. Pedro's space does not experience geometrical limits. It is like entering an alphabet soup nuclear war. The poem attacks the central nervous system:

> do not let
> artificial lamps
> make strange shadows
> out of you
> do not dream
> if you want your dreams
> to come true.

There is no outside protection:

> your breath
> is your promiseland
> if you want
> to feel very rich
> look at your hands
> that is where
> the definition of magic
> is located at.

Lucky CienFuegos places the center of safety smack in the middle of his "I." In "My In Of Me" the reader is pulled by a whirl of energy that grows as he realizes that

> my in of me will always be by, for he
> or I, one of us will be there for this is I
> I saw through the windows of this skull.

Sandra Esteves' "i am the bird in transit for the winter," not included in this collection, defines the "i" as the point of reference for all understanding. She sees herself as the

> . . . eagle flying high
> and the egg shaping life.

She makes the "i" the center stone, the grinding stone. She is the place from where all definitions of self in time and place evolve:

> i am the timeless
> and spaceless
>
> the burning
> and freezing
> the smallest
> and greatest
>
> i am love

A dusmic poem fortifies and centralizes the reader. It gives hope without deceptive illusions. Sandra knows that between man and woman exists the possibility of balance. In "for tito" she achieves a beautiful energy-giving balance. The ugly (the ghetto) blends with the beautiful (their love) and the result is rich with love:

> together
> we reap mystical sugarcane in the ghetto
> where all the palm trees grow ripe
> and rich with coconut milk.

The poems in this section are poems of love. But the eye is kept sharp. It is a love that grows out of desperation, strength, and a genuine confidence in the self.

Miguel Algarín

for tito

you, macho machete
are all the fine conga rhythms
played on the street, in parties, in spring
all the beautiful vibes of la playa sextet
washing up against the palms in the hairs of my back
turning my blood into salsa
and filling me up inside to swell
with who i am

you, macho paciencia
are the star of my aqua sea

and when there are no more sunsets
and i become alone and lost
it is your brown hands holding me steady
around my waist
to move and sway with

you, macho soledad
are a unique language
the one filling my eyes with heat for you
growing and pounding
with all the desire
of your drum
pounding with my womb
planting seeds in the night

together
we reap mystical sugarcane in the ghetto
where all the palm trees grow ripe
and rich with coconut milk.

Sandra María Esteves

Blanket Weaver

weaver
weave us a song of many threads

weave us a red of fire and blood
that taste of sweet plum
fishing around the memories of the dead
following a scent wounded
our spines bleeding with pain

weave us a red of passion
that beats wings against a smoky cloud
and forces motion into our lungs

weave us a song
of yellow and gold and life itself
that lights a way through wildgrowth
burned in pain
aged with steady conviction
with bunions callouses and leathered hides

weave us into the great magnetic center
pulling your fingers into topaz canyons
a single lonely web glitters like a flash of thunder
your thumb feeling into my womb
placing sweatseeds of floral honey
into continuous universal suspension

weave us a song of red and yellow
and brown
that holds the sea and the sky in its skin
that holds the bird and mountain in its voice
that builds upon our graves a home
for injustice fear oppression abuse and disgrace
and upon these fortifications
of strength unity and direction

weave us a song to hold us
when the wind blows so cold to make our children wail

submerged in furious ice
a song pure and raw
that burns paper
and attacks the colorless venom stalking hidden
in the petal soft sweetness of the black night

weave us a rich round black that lives
in the eyes of our warrior child
and feeds our mouths with moon breezes
with rhythms interflowing
through all spaces of existence
a black that holds the movement of eternity

weave us a song for our bodies to sing

weave us a song of many threads
that will dance with the colors of our people
and cover us with the warmth of peace

Sandra María Esteves

i look for peace great graveyard

i look for peace great graveyard
new york spits my eye
oil dragged hummingbird, is there no peace
sometimes i want to die i feel just die

bedroom walls bare stagnant water
drenched colorless laugh
the same voice haunting pillowcase
the same the same i have no face
or bones to hold my walk

what do i know of men
enough to slave myself for pickings
empty nude and sleepless
abortion without
for all of what for what?
is there peace

the meat is rotting fast inside
my womb disintegrates in anal slurs
hopes tied in metal flavor ribbon
tied to kill the dream born with mother
tied to kill the child within
tied around my hands frozen fresh daily

when will earth cease renovation
trees are where i wish to live
and play the dance of chinese wind chimes
hear the ancient pipe the breath
that touches my eyes to see

Sandra María Esteves

Sunday, August 11, 1974

Sunday afternoon and it is one-thirty and all the churchgoing
latinos have crossed themselves and are now going home to share
in the peace of the day, pan y mantequilla, una taza de café and many
sweet recollections of el rinconcito en Juncos, donde Carmencita,
María y Malén jugaban y peleaban.

Sunday afternoon and it is one-thirty and all the
churchgoing latinos fuse each other with love and the women dress
so clean and pure and the children walk so straight and pure and the
fathers look so proud and pure and everything so right and pure and
even as I wake up to my nephew's voice coming through the window,
there is pleasure in awakening. My mother and father and Grafton and
Johnny come in, there is light in
their eyes,
there is pleasure in living,
there is no shame in being
full of love,
there is no shame in being
nude while my mother's
eyes look in at me,
looking at my nude body,
body that she made mixing her blood
with my father's,
and there's no rushing for clothes
just sweet openness in being
loved by my family.
Sunday afternoon and it is
one-thirty and all the churchgoing latinos have crossed themselves
and my body swings free.

Miguel Algarín

San Juan/an arrest /Maguayo/
a vision of Malo dancing

The VW breaks down on
the highway and we seek
a mechanic. We are given
directions and what we're
finding out is that
"it's nice to live in fear"
fear of police, fear of being
caught masturbating, fear,
fear of being caught,
apprehended, tu entiendes?
fear of having to answer
the questions of the law.
We were on our way
to Cupey after having been
in San Juan
¡no!
¡esperate! it was the other
way around. We had just
arrived. Lucky saw a woman,
he felt he pitied her
but really it was a queso jones
that got us into a scrap
with the cops—we thought
that getting off the plane
would drop us into the lap
of "la familia," we thought
we'd find a noble feeling
that we'd be sure and secure
that there would be a madre
alma to kiss our New York
soot-filled bodies and soul
pero cuando el policía
asked "where's your license?"
I said hey I've come to see
Borinquen to love her shores
to spread my beauty here

my NUYORICAN being
my eagle knife caution
filled mind reads your neon
signs AQUÍ YOUR CREDITO ES GOOD
and I feel sad that in school,
we're forced to reach for standards
do you know what I mean?
standards like
> STANDARD ENGLISH
> STANDARD SPANISH

but meanwhile your neon
signs tell the real truth:
you are bilingual Puerto Rico
you are NUYORICAN on
your own home soil,
your schools scold me for illiteracy
while your Cuban/American bankers
sell me the island in spanglish
(SPANGLISH-NUYORICAN)
and that's the truth
of the dollar matter
the conscience of Borinquen
is a spanish/english
neon nightmare
but really it is all about
getting caught and having
to admit my license has
expired—"you're under
arrest" pero señor Policía
I am on Borinquen and my
license is a fault of law
but I am clean so let
me go and I'll send you
a poem—"you're under
arrest" twenty-five dollars later and much
humiliation we called it a draw

and I was free to go—but
Lucky it was, sure enough
lucky, wasn't it? the
cop's eyes burned holes
through your clothes
the cop x-rayed your soul
but you were quicker
than god before his creation,
how beautiful when you
dropped your sack and the
papers spilled over the
street and the grass was
in among the papers and
as you handed the cop your
sack you pulled the
papers together keeping
our ganga out of sight
how smooth
how easy it was
to keep our secret
yet how fast
how cunning
you were
when you shifted
your eyes from street to sack
to street to yourself standing
holding our weed between
the pages of your poems
and how clear it was
that el policía's eyes
couldn't x-ray the poems,
he couldn't
defeat the POEMS
he couldn't discover
our innocent smoke secret,
smooth,

cunning,
fast,
deliberate,
inside the self
that's what the street
Nuyorican has to learn
for survival and that's
what Lucky knows—
he knows salvation is from inside
the self—
Maguayo home of el
jibaro Puertoriqueño your
conscience, the smell of your
smartness is molded, born,
grown, nourished in the streets
of New York: in the Bon Soir
I see the energies of our nation
pour its sweat juice as
peals of electronic sounds pour
over sweated bodies
I see brown women being
brown women to pussydom
desiring, inventing the
deep down liberation of
being woman and in love
with woman—Butch and
the Sun-Dance Chick—
Borinquen your beautiful
brown women love each other
in the public eye of the Bon Soir
as Malo's sweat
bathes each male eye
with wonder that his beautiful
masculinity can contort itself
in telling the dance tale
of the city—

City of New York
Malo tells the story of your
factory slaving police
intimidated working class,
each step enacts the work-
aday sexual torture of the
slums and your beautiful
boys without Christian Parents
to sustain them in false virtue,
Malo the tortured electronic
sound of black America
becomes apple-pie cheddar
cheese wisdom to my eyes—
I see you are high on moving
faster than sight
I see your right leg
curl up to your waist
as you spread both hands
and sprint off your left leg—
Malo do you see?
that that's the position your
factory-slave forefathers
have held as they've worked
the machinery of the city—
spin into hysteria
dance the working class roots
of your muscles into telling
the humiliation of your people
through motion—dance
and torture the air, writhe
your body into despair,
into the joy of dancing
out our pain/your pain
as well:
Maguayo
campo campo terrestre

de Puerto Rico
your children speak an English-
Spanish mixed salad,
the vulgar language of
the spirit that is to be.
Maguayo gracias por Lucky
and muchas, muchas
gracias for letting me feel
the soil of this island without
the neon lights of
north american night-
mare dream of TVs in every
bathroom
Maguayo
gracias por las letrinas
that connect my shit to myself
without the sanitary mania that
now rules our lives
Maguayo
te quiero porque los aguacates
cuestan quince chavos
Maguayo you were and are
the proof of our lost innocence,
of our impurity,
Maguayo we hardly own you
we barely make you our own
maybe
maybe
when Malo dances on your soil
your holy baptism will
make you ours
to own
to keep
to build on—
Maguayo
the mosquitoes have bred
on your soil

after two weeks of rain,
they rape my soft skin,
they invade my fluids,
they suck my pores
free of the blood that I am
to offer,
me comen vivo,
me deboran la sangre,
there's something capitalistic
about mosquitoes: they feed till
they almost burst full of blood
and then they go on to seek
new survival energy,
to draw more blood elsewhere.
Maguayo your jibaro,
your survival
is Nuyorican not Taino,
not black, not white
just Nuyorican—
I'll tell you something more
Borinquen
as I sat all ñagotao there
in Maguayo
as I let my intestines have free
flow and as my constipation
won I realized I was just as
afraid in Borinquen
as I am in New York
pero te quiero Maguayo
porque los aguacates
cuestan quince chavos
te amo por la simplicidad
que le ofreces
a uno who lives in
524 E. 6th St.
New York, New York
          10009

My first night in Maguayo
began in a VW and
ended in a bed sleeping
three: Dadi, Miky and myself,
we slept easy till the morning
heat sent a fever of itch
to be up at the beach getting sun,
sun for my psyche,
sun for my skin,
sun for my nourishment,
sun for my vision—
the water at Boquerón is bath-
tub warm,
it touches gently,
the waves at Boquerón are light
gentle invasions,
the water is gentle,
the water seduces,
the water accommodates
itself around my balls
around the whole of my body,
at Boquerón six kilometers from
Maguayo the sensual truth
is that the waves seduce,
the waves arouse my cock,
the waves gently lick
the head of my free swinging
cock, the gentle knocks
on my head erect me,
the gentle sea waves
ebb and flow around my body
the whole of the Caribbean Sea
moves to the rhythm of my
opening pores
my blood stiffens my cock
my ass is in spasms

the waves move to the rhythms
of my spinal cord
unleashing centers of passion
that squeeze my sperm
up / through to the head,
the moves are quick
the sea is gentle
the breeze caresses
my spine jerks hard
my cock skin stretches
to the rhythm of the sea—
the sea's a ring around my rosie
and I am the father of the
oceans as my sperm
swims right up into
the world's wide open SEAS.

Miguel Algarín

i feel the eve

i feel the eve
of my body
flowing through
the cycle of woman.
blood rush down
cleanse my womb.
my hair at motion,
limbs in stimulation,
effecting sensation,
submerging in love.

Luz Rodriguez

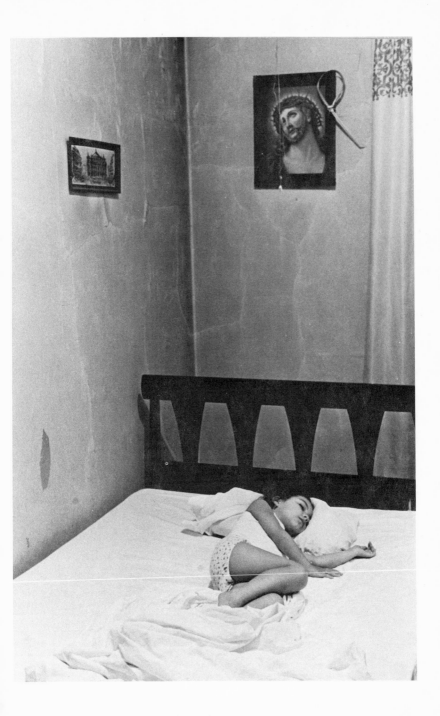

Holding You

You taste like a big round orange sun on the still
  ocean . . .
    . . . a peaceful seagull gliding by.
You smell like running through wet green grass
  smelling the pureness of all that's green . . .
    . . . diving into a rushing waterfall
     biting into a crisp green apple.

Luz Rodriguez

do not let

do not let
artificial lamps
make strange shadows
out of you
do not dream
if you want your dreams
to come true
you knew how to sing
before you was
issued a birth certificate
turn off the stereo
this country gave you
it is out of order
your breath
is your promiseland
if you want
to feel very rich
look at your hands
that is where
the definition of magic
is located at

Pedro Pietri

Voodoo

the blood on the clock
is dead serious
no glass
      just eyes
to avoid incorrections
, the sounds you
      did not hear
was probably somebody
talking to their self
without saying a word
, the other day
      we answered
the door after hearing
somebody knock
and nobody was there
, this happens every day
      around here
, we let whoever it was
enter and leave
      because we
need all the empty space
we have available
for those who are
      interested
in being seen

Pedro Pietri

The Influence of Don Quixote

Screws screwing spinning twirling the mind moving
the mood of time with looney tunes transforming humans
into cartoons. Cold frozen ice cubes bathing themselves
in the veins of Don Quixote. The vibrating . . . brating
guitar strings, and the Chicano verbal rhythms which
rewind the laughs and giggles of living room time. Shares
the wine and inhales the welcome of Chicanos arrived,
together they share the universal rubberbands, within
moments stringing bilingual itchy fingers created a
chicano band. Giggling kickiling Don Quixote rushing
to the brain. Now I wonder if there are any midnight
cowboys under the influence of Don Quixote? Wine perfuming
the living room of time. Midnight cowboys awake with their
weekend blues, and Santa María weeps between the echoing
tears of love. Along waits the squeaking far far foreign
roads which keep you awake and you even see dawn squeaking
through the firmament. Rust of dust rushing into the lid
of your eyes. Dreaming sleeping minds that hover over
as gentle as butterflies. And when awakened the world is
your stage. The caravan minds which travel with a blow
of wind and cut through the brickminded with their theatrical
rhythms of truth and love which glides on truth. Humble
are the hearts that wish they could bathe in the mouth of the
ocean. Instead they are spit out. But strong they are
and continue the glide of the theatrical caravan minds.

Lucky CienFuegos

High heel, silver shoes

The sounds of high-heeled silver shoes
click clock click clock
as squeaking giggles squeaked to the earth at night
Jennifer, the wilderness of my universe
the emotional feelings that travel through my cosmos
that shine in the starless nights
because I am the wisest mist
that stroked with all the might
the purity of I may not be so bright
but to I who is dark
purity in me don't shine
neither is hard to define
if you're longing to try
you'll catch me on the stride
My love the world real
is the so many I's
feelings is the storyteller of humanity
even the drums of the moment
they speak with feelings
and the silence responds in peace
Magical thankful is I
who now thanks the moving force
of a pen so gently being caressed
as it maneuvers and tries
with all his might
it is I the pen
that describes this poem
Earthly may be the nights
when the planets will no longer shine

when it is too late to claim right
but who am I to tell you wrong from right
One day when your cosmos flips and twirls
and when you lie gently on your loft
that's when perhaps minds give
birth to comprehension
Ha ha
ha ha ha ha
squeaking is the feelings that so suddenly
ha ha ha ha ahahahahahahhh
crashes in a planet haahaahaah
'scuse me, it was a tickle in the gut.
I depart with planets at twirl.

Lucky CienFuegos

Dedicada a María Rodriguez Martínez
February 24, 1975

Te admiro y te quiero madre mía

El collar de rosa
rosa de lila querida
madre mía
hoy enfrente de tí
demuestro mi cariño
sin bacilón
sin miedo espero
en un camino
la lluvia con sus gotas frías
y el viento sin deseos
de acariciar
y los vientos de los cielos,
cielo alma corazón
espero el día de mi porfía
hoy me fijo en tí
madre mía
enferma y siempre con
la sonrisa
madre mía debajo de esa risa
conozco el dolor
pero hoy será el recuerdo
de los mañanas
fíjense, mírenme
sobre mi tumba no quiero rosas frías
querida madre mía

te amo, me recuerdo
los helados fríos de mi juventud,
cuando niño mi helado
los dos gozábamos
y todos los sábados
son como la claridad
y también como ese
sentimiento que viene
con la porfía de la claridad
collar de rosa
rosa lila
lealtad siempre será madre mía
y si la grama del mañana
arropa sus pájaros
con recuerdos de hoy
espero el día
madre mía.

Lucky CienFuegos

Dedicated to María Rodriguez Martínez
February 24, 1975

I admire and love you mother

Rose necklace
lilac rose beloved
mother
today in front of you
I show my love
without hesitation
without fear
on the road
the rain and its cold drops
and the wind without the will
to caress
the sky winds
sky, soul heart
I wait for the day of my struggle
today I think of you
my mother
sick but always
with a smile
Mother underneath that smile
I know the pain
but today will be the memory
of tomorrows
pay attention, look at me
above my tomb I do not want cold roses
beloved mother
I love you, I remember
the cold ice creams of my youth,
when I was a child

we'd both enjoy my ice cream
and Saturdays
are like clarity
and like that
feeling that comes
with the struggle for clarity
rose necklace
lilac rose
loyalty forever mother
and if tomorrow's grass
cloaks its birds
with memories of today
I await that day
Mother.

Lucky CienFuegos
(translation by *Miguel Algarín*)

The Nerve of Time

The nerve of time has inhaled the veins of fear
greenish eyes tremble within their sockets
she drifts with the cloud of yellowness
negative was the echoing fear which cries in silence
and moves on with melancholy blues
perhaps you left with a thought that I would
cripple the sounds of love
or liquidate the desires of tomorrows
Fear me not for I will not awake the sleeping sorrows
neither caress the shadows of unjust
thick is the wind that lays before you
Sceptical—Scepticalist is the down obstacles
in your everyday seconds which forces force
upon self
Release the thing, Thee
chase the blues out the window
the many underestimate the air of wisdom birth
which caress with feathers of sorrows
but strong is the self that melts the feathers
and purifies and converts into wings of love
so remove the forces which force mental castles
upon the cells of indoctrination
clarifications clarify the nerve of time.

Lucky CienFuegos

My In of Me

In a poem I wrote were these lines
        and Daydreams just sits by and admires
        his dreamers.
But I reversed that for it is I even if I die
me or I will always be dear and surely open ears
even if I die my in of me will always hear hahahahaha
for if I die I will always be recalled
for memories will awaken the conversations
still being repeated as time tears and rots
you to death but I reverse for they will
always recall of me, even if it's bad,
even if its good, even if they say, "Mother fuck you"
I, neither do I care of the remarks they make of me
because is something of me which is a seed
I planted in them in all which I have met
the seed right there and then was planted
for I am the planet, cheer, laugh if you desire,
but it is I that will always be recalled
even if they are spoken through hypocrisy
but I will always be there even if I die
my in of me will always be by, for he
or I, one of us will be there for this is I
I saw through the windows of this skull.

Lucky CienFuegos

Nocturnos en una Noche Perdida

Voces a lo lejos
             el comienzo de una vida
entre paredes del pecho
             de un niño en su pobresa
un grito abierto
             un paso a la muerte

¿Que será la muerte?
                       ¿Será realidad?
O será un paso a la eternidad
Una risa oculta
             y adolorida
de una madre en espera
que con sus lágrimas
             sella
la carta para su hijo
Voces que vienen
                       de la profundidad del río
Decidme que sucedió con las cenisas
                       escondidas
y las siluetas de los poetas
             en busca
de un poema escondido y desconocido

Noche agria y llena de tristezas
             en tí me fijo
             con una esperanza
             con un olvido, quizás
noche no vés que,
             tus latidos me llaman

Derramados los sentidos
el sereno convertido
en un mar de estrellas
noche serena y angustiada
decidme que ha sido
de la madrugada apretada
en las manos de una pareja
Que con sus ojos ciegos
buscan un silencio   lo prohibido

Desfigurado el destino
    dos palomas en el aire
un sereno ajeno
    en un mundo
    en la obscuridad
un quejido . . . una suplica
la risa de una niña
y en sus manos
    esconde
    un retrato
    y un cerrillo prendido
una viejita hablando . . .
    con el rocío
un matrimonio en desastre . . .
y la agonía de los padres

No se puede pretender el fuego de la
        Tierra
ni tampoco resolver
    una mañana sin sangre
pero sí   devolver . . .
    una libertad negada
y hacer con el rosario
    un sueño de la nada

Lo tienes todo
    y lo tiras al vacío
    y con las miradas de misterio

busco las huellas en los arrabales

Y tu sabes de las angustias de esa noche
  yo dormido en los vagones
    del subterraneo
    soñé con la risa
      de una criatura
    en su juego con las lagartijas
Vivo y no lo parezco
    en una depresión disimulada

con una sonrisa vaga
en un altar lejano
estréchame la mano hermano;
y unámonos en la lucha
y quizás en el destierro
y en el retorno de los paisajes
vendrá el sumbido agudo
de la gente de las calles
¡Y hubo mucha gente!
Me decías tú que fue ahí
en donde te confundieron
con las flores
te confieso que me sucedió lo mismo
te confundí con una rosa
que caía de los cielos
rodeada por angelitos negros

Corazón destrozado
no hay imposible
si reina el amor
Hubo un riachuelo cerca del sol
marcado . . .
y un suspiro del ayer
que a mi brindó
tus ojos, cascabel
flor del río
y seguí desafiando el continuar
del envenenado frío
y el mal aliento del odiar
por un retoño mío
las palabras injertas
pero impedido yo no podría quedarme
Conservadas están las súplicas ya muertas de las gallinas
retozando
Tres figuras marchan   al compas del viento
y las voces unidas en coro   quieren unir un verso
que se hunde en el nocturno   de esta inesperada
y moribunda noche . . .

Carlos Conde

Nocturne on a Lost Night

Voices in the distance
            the beginning of a life
between the walls of the chest
            of a child in his poverty
an open scream
            a step towards death

what will death be?
            will it be reality?
or will it be a step into eternity
a laugh hidden
            and pained
of a mother in waiting
who with her tears
            seals
the letter for her son
voices that come
            from the depth of the river
tell me what happened to the ashes
            hidden
and the poet's shadows
            in search
of a hidden and unknown poem

Sour night filled with sadness
            I watch you
            with hope
            with abandonment, maybe
you do not see that,
            your throbbing calls me

my senses spill
the evening converted
into a sea of stars
calm and anguished night
tell me what happened
to the dawn held tightly in the hands of a couple
that with blind eyes
search for silence   prohibited

disfigured destiny
                two pigeons in the air
an alien calm
                in a world
                in obscurity
lament . . . supplication
a child's laughter
and in her hands
                she hides a picture
                a lit cigarette
an old woman talking . . .
                with the dew
a marriage on the rocks . . .
and the agony of the parents

you can not wish fire from earth
nor resolve
                a morning without blood
but you can return . . .
                a denied liberty
and construct with a rosary
                a dream out of nothing.

You have everything
                and you throw it into nothingness
                and with mysterious looks

I search for clues in the slums

and you know about the anguish of that night
        I   slept in subway cars
                dreamt of the laughter
                of a young child
                as it played with salamanders

I live but it doesn't seem it
                in a hidden depression
with a weak smile

in a distant altar
lend me your hand brother
and let us write in the struggle
in the recurrence of landscapes
will come the acute murmur
of street people

and there were many people!
You used to tell that it was there
where they confused you
with the flowers
I confess to you that the same happened to me
I took you for a rose
that fell from the sky
surrounded by little black angels

Destroyed heart
nothing is impossible
if love reigns
There was a little brook near the sun
marked . . .
and in yesterday's sigh
your eyes celebrated me
flowering jungle of the river
and I continued to defy
the poisonous cold
and hate's bad breath
through a sprout of mine
the grafted words
but I could not be restrained
The cries of the dead chickens are preserved
romping
three figures marching to the tune of the wind
and the voices a chorus want to unite in a verse
that sinks in the nocturne of this unexpected
moribund night . . .

Carlos Conde
(translation by *Miguel Algarín*)

Prison Love

When i last slept with you
      stroke after stroke
         was like a eucharist
            on a sunday mass—
               so soothering to the guilty spirit
               so dry on the throat . . .
The sweat of two erotic gods
      soaked our Brown bodies
         with the moisture
           of an exotic island
             going under
               a doubtful sea of love . . .
From your womb
      dropped tears of lust
         captured by my desires
           with mellow thrusts
             on counting speed
               while we sung
                  a song of hungery love
                    abandoned to a raving climax . . .
By each other we laid
      tired
         and while waiting for a rusty breeze
         you threw your leg
           atop my body
             and said "papi que polvo"
               while i smiled wryly
                  thinking i had done something . . .
Relaxed
      we faced each other again
         laughing and carrying on
           like two little kids
             and you said "papi i luv yu"
               and i said "sí mami lo sé"
               never was you to know
               how much i pained

from knowing
you really meant it . . .
I caress your prolific thighs
you parted your lips
once again my tongue was to nourish
from your beautiful Brown eyes
your cute tender nose
your natural pink lips—
while a dream was monitored
on an erected cold prison sheet . . .
Lower . . . lower
your bosom
your belly
even your belly button was too much to resist
the sweat of your thighs
so salty
so rich
you cried "no, no"
i turned you around
up and down your back
my tongue worked
over . . . around . . . and in
your buttox . . . i was there . . .
Tenderly i turned you back around
kissing at your legs
playing with my nose on you
you wiggled
and then
my tongue was all over your sweet pussy
while you said "no papi no me lavao"
but you still spread
them long slender legs . . .
The sounds of love
were all thru that mystic Ghetto room
which now ran an instant replay
in a sensual dream

169

                    of an eloping
                        prisoner . . .
        Then only to feel me go into you
                as never before
                    and while your fingertips sank into my back
                    you yelled at the top of your lungs
                        never to let you go
                            cause the peak was near
                                oh so near
                                    that i thrusted and you stroked
                                    and as two erupting volcanos
                                        "mami . . . mami"
                                            "papi . . . papi" . . .
I can still hear you
from within these prison walls
"papi . . . papi"
but the sounds were so faint
my bars vibrated a lost
but
i still got up
to clean myself
with a smile . . .
                        (when two slept together but one got up)

T. C. Garcia

Water Figure

Escaping from last to present vehicle
Keeping in pace with longines accuracy
Swung around to point of destination
Before me two fair maidens, approaching
transfer point.

Moving from counterpart of house
Hastily pondering at figure
Stunned, joyed at vision
Daydreaming, happily at water
cohort

Signify Egyptian hieroglyphic, in
twentieth century
replica of pharaoh head
Long star texan cowpoke
European ballerina dancer

Resting, inbedded in grave, flowing
graciously with juice
Mirror reflecting life secrets

Jest tales of beginners to present
Specter, but sincere to beholder
keen sight

Fierce curiosity, distorted mind
but gratified at spectacle
Sitting, drawing, fitting sections
used and new

Still unaware of happening, but facing
it reality
Presume puzzle, wishing for recurrence
if heard.

Isidro Garcia

Bruja

(A tropical/jungle plant that grows in
Puerto Rico. It is very thick & heavy.
A single leaf of this plant can be
taken anywhere, resoiled, and a new plant
will grow from it. Each leaf is seeded.
Bruja also means Witch.)

a plastic Bruja
fell
from a 4th floor windowsill
against the cold concrete
of sidewalks
that describe this metal city.
it did not break.
but it will not grow
this plastic flower that is store-bought
impersonating Spirits
that are real.
no it will not grow.
it is not real in that way
in that respect.

now had it been a Bruja from Puerto Rico
broken-away from the join of its family
beneath trees & rocks
in jungles
of birds that sing
& animals
that crawl within the dirt
& eat the fruits that grow from trees/
had that Bruja that fell
come from where the Sun sinks close enough
to touch the trees
& be blessed as a Natural God
(unlike airplanes)
had that Bruja that fell against the concrete
been one of those
the same that grow
on Doña Juana's windowsill

the ones that she brought back
from her last trip to the Island
the one about her father's death   there
her plants grow
in all colors of the Sun & Moon
& in all seasons of this Earth & stretch
to enter onto the walls
that make her home/
had that fallen Bruja been one of those
it would have dug its hole
in through that concrete that is man-made
& found itself a home
deep   ﹅
where the Earth is warm again
& soon
it would have grown between the cracks
the Sun makes when it's hot
& it would have joined the flowers
of colors that are different
& that have come to meet
on this battlefield of concrete
& then
that same Bruja that once felt
the cold of steel & asphalt
it would have raised its hand
to throw its brick
too.

Jesús Papoleto Meléndez

Una Lágrima en un Cristal

Una lágrima en un Cristal
cayendo little by little como
las gotas de la fire pompa
que suena en la noche
con su ritmo diciendo
injusto-injusto-injusto

Una lágrima en un Cristal
que abosteza los llantos
de las madres
con sus hijos en Vietnam
porque ellas son las que están
en el wrongside

Una lágrima en un Cristal
desnuda el espíritu del tecato
al ver su cuerpo en un espejo
y al ver su vida en una callejera sin salida
con sus brazos, su alma y su needle sangrante

Una lágrima en un Cristal
paredes de prisión en la mente
de hombres libres . . .
fiebre que besa la sangre de las mujeres
tired de ser no más que objetos sexuales . . .

Una lágrima en un Cristal
la risa en los ojos del jurado
sequestran las últimas palabras del juez
el último sonido de la calle
último beso de your old lady
el abrazo del niño

Una lágrima en un Cristal
la botánica del espiritísmo
lástima el birth del pobre baby
justicia en las canciones del poeta
envenenado con anger-rubia

Una lágrima en un Cristal
bendito sea dios—tenga compasión
desrrama compasión en la frente
de los sacerdotes that aprecian las flores
de lata and oraciones de plastic

Una lágrima en un Cristal
tocando los lips del maestro Albizu
la saliva de cristo
Una lágrima en un Cristal
has fallen y se ha entregado a la tierra . . .

Miguel Piñero

A Tear in the Mirror

A tear in the mirror
falling little by little like
drops from a fire pump
echoing through the night crying
the rhythms of Injustice-Injustice-Injustice

A tear in the mirror
that yawns the wailing
of mothers
with sons in Vietnam
because they are the ones
on the wrong side

A tear in the mirror
undress the spirit of a junkie
who sees his body in the mirror
and his life on a dead end street
with his arms, his soul and his needle
bloody

A tear in the mirror
prison walls in the minds
of free men
fever kissing the blood of women
tired of being nothing more than sexual
objects

A tear in the mirror
laughter in the jury's eyes
kidnaps the last words of the judge
the last sound of the streets
the last kiss from your old lady
the embrace of a child

A tear in the mirror
the botánica of spiritualism
the pain in the birth of a poor baby
songs of justice from the poet
filled with anger

A tear in the mirror
God have pity—have compassion
pour compassion on the foreheads
of priests that appreciate the flowers
of tin and plastic prayers

A tear in the mirror
touch the lips of the teacher Albizu
the saliva of christ
A tear in the mirror
has fallen and has integrated
with the earth

Miguel Piñero

The Records of Time

Two hundred fifty million years ago, long before the recorded history
of man, someone sat down and recorded it; And this man's name was
Time, and so it was only right that he should call his writings
"records" and add his name to history. Time, a young and ambitious
energy, lived in the summer hills of the Antarctic. He lived near a wise
old gentleman named His Story and his wife Truth, and their two sons
Hypocrisy and Reality. Truth was a very blunt woman who always
tried her best to please all her family and friends, and being such a
pleasing woman, she always ended up on the bottom of the list and
was chosen by His Story to be in the kitchen doing dirty dishes. At
places she would try to get away from the kitchen and take Reality
for a day at the amusement center. Though she loved her family
equally, she had a certain affection for Reality, because everyone
in the community was afraid of him (for reasons known only to
Unknown, a distant uncle) and she always tried her most to be with
him to comfort his loneliness. But that was only once in three
lifecycles that she would enjoy taking Reality in hand and walk on
the beaches of the North Lifeantic ocean and the earth would shake
with pleasure, as well as pain for both of them—Pain was there only
because Earth had some wild notion that there's pain in pleasure and
so on. Once Truth and Reality were about to leave the house to
buy a new set of garments of the spring. His Story caught them at
the door with faithful Hypocrisy at his right side (they were more like
brothers under the skin than like Father and son.) They began to
accuse them of not loving them enough, and to give foundation
to their argument, they enlisted the aide of the poker-playing buddies,
Shame, Guilt, and Complexes. Reality ran out the door, and Truth
stayed behind after much verbal abuse. She succumbed to their will
and hid the dirty laundry. That night feeling very relieved of a
heavy burden His Story and Hypocrisy spent the night at Coward's
Bar & Grill where they celebrated their chained freedom, drinking lies
and making passionate love to the whore Cheat. This is where His
Story met Time. With the fumes of lies in their heads, Time and His
Story became pretty good companions. They all sat around listening
to Hypocrisy tell tales. Greed and Opportunity, two men who shared
the work of the lower forty's, had stepped in through the door and

179

picking up on the good vibes surrounding the table of His Story, bought a round of lies for the group and stood drugged at the words of Hypocrisy, a heavy rapper—in fact his nickname was Quibber with the Jibbers. Opportunity hit upon an idea on how to become immortal and ran it to Greed who told His Story and Hypocrisy, and Time was jotting it all down for his records. Simultaneously they saw Reality passing by the front of Coward's window display and fought among each other for the richness of it all. His Story having the most intelligence and just plain good old game, told them that he had the secret of immortality and that there was only room for one more in the zone of immortality. Being a fair man, he declared that whoever came to his house with the largest number of followers would share the bed with the secret of immortality, his wife Truth. Greed, Opportunity, and Hypocrisy jumped out of their chairs and raced out the door in a mad dash for followers, circling the globe a million ways in charades. Hypocrisy crawled, Greed took to the winds, Opportunity sailed the seas, while His Story laughed at the tears his wife Truth would shed, and time—well Time, he just stood still. . . .

Miguel Piñero

AFTERWORD

A poem describes the neighborhood of the writer for the reader. There are poems, or rather, there are poets who describe conditions that are either in the past or in the future. The poems in this anthology are in the dance of the moment. The Nuyorican poets have worked to establish the commonplace because they have wanted to locate their position on earth, the ground, the neighborhood, the environment. These are the places that the poet names for his readers. To cut into the immediate moment and deliver an image of what is going on and then move on so that the next image is fresh and alert to the ever-changing present is the business of the poet.

Once the qualities of the space in which we live are defined by the poets, the next step for communicating meaning is to establish the action of the poem. What is it that is going on? The poem has to satisfy both these needs if it is to have a common ground on which to move its feelings:

> Before the beginning
> God created God
> In the beginning
> God created the ghettos and slums
> and God saw this was good.
> So God said,
> "Let there be more ghettos & slums"
> and there were more ghettos & slums.
> But God saw this was plain
> so
> to decorate it
> God created leadbase paint . . .
>   ("The Book of Genesis According to
>   Saint Miguelito" by Miguel
>   Piñero)

Piñero goes to the beginning and there, in common grounds, he creates the bible of the slums. Saint Miguelito sermonizes that God is eternal in his infinite errors. Saint Miguelito has a sense of humor. The reader is not thrown into fear over the absence of right. Instead, Saint Miguelito concentrates the reader into his moment.

Once the common ground and action of the poem are established, then what the poem becomes is the event of itself. The poem makes you pay attention, and makes you care. It is the moment that imprints a cultural presence upon the world. Nuyorican poetry is the talk of the ongoing. It is the event of the moment.

Miguel Algarín

Biographies

Miguel Algarín, born in Santurce, Puerto Rico, is Assistant Professor of English Literature at Livingston College, Rutgers University. He is the translator of Pablo Neruda's *Canción de Gesta (A Song of Protest)* which is soon to be published by William Morrow & Company. Mr. Algarín directs the Nuyorican Playwrights'/Actors' Workshop, which was formed to develop playwrights and actors simultaneously. He is also the author of *Olú Clemente*, which was performed at the Delacorte Theater in the summer of 1973. He recently completed his third book of poetry, *Mongo Affair* and is currently working on a novel.

Miguel Gomez Piñero was born in Gurabo, Puerto Rico on December 19, 1946. He is self-educated and was raised on the Lower East Side of New York City. He is a prize-winning poet and playwright, the receiver of the New York Drama Critics Circle Award and the Obie (Off-Broadway) and was an Antoinette Perry (Tony) Award nominee, 1974-1975.

Piñero is a member of Actors Equity Associaton, and of the Dramatists Guild and the Authors League of America. His work is now being studied in various universities and colleges throughout the nation and South America.

Both Algarín and Piñero live and work on the Lower East Side of New York City.

Gil Mendez was born in New York's Spanish Harlem in 1947, the youngest of seven children. His family subsequently moved to the South Bronx where he spent most of his youth and became interested in photography. Most of the photographs in *Nuyorican Poetry* stem from this period physically as well as spiritually.

Gil Mendez is self-taught in photography. He was graduated from Livingston College, Rutgers University, in 1974, where he also taught a course in introductory photography.

He is currently in New Mexico working on material for a photographic essay on Mexican-Americans.